SERVICE

MY WORDS. MY LIFE. MY TRUTH.

Bible references from the New American Standard Bible
ISBN-13: 978-1979357555
ISBN-10: 1979357552

CreateSpace
Available from Amazon.com and other retail outlets Available on Kindle and other devices

Written by Isaac Carree
Content and Interior by Nations28/Kandice Phillips
Cover Graphics by Justin Foster
Cover Photo by Alex D. Rogers

Executive Assistant: Chidonna Kardar, Fashion Consultant: Tawana "Tee" Anderson/Dressed to a Tee,
Jacket: Melissa A. Mitchell/Abeille Creations, Grooming: Timothy Rogers, Road Manager: Kevin King

SERVICE

MY WORDS. MY LIFE. MY TRUTH.

ISAAC CARREE

DEDICATION
FROM THE BOTTOM OF MY HEART

Wow, let me be honest with you, I fought writing this book for 6 years, because I felt like my story wasn't interesting enough to share. But I can honestly admit that I haven't had peace for 6 years because I did not obey the voice of the Lord concerning this matter. So, to be at this stage where I'm actually writing this book has once again shown the awesome wonders of God!

I'm not writing this book because I have all the answers or because I've accomplished all there is to accomplish, but I wrote this book to inspire, uplift and encourage people like me who've been through hell and back and wanted to give up but in the process found their passion by unselfishly serving. So, this book is not from a place of triumphs. Triumphs build ego, its valleys and downfalls build character. This is about the opposite of ego, it's about how you bounce back through serving. This is what I want people to get from this book, I was blessed by this quote by my brother DeVon Franklin "You must carry a crown, before you can wear one". Translation: so many people want success overnight, they want to rush it, they want to microwave it, they want the crown, they want the throne, but they don't want the process. That process is SERVICE! What you make happen for someone else, God will make happen for you. So, I dedicate this book to all my fellow servants who wear that title with humility, honor and pride. God sees you, so stop looking for approval from other people.

I want to take this time to thank my family. To my wife Dietra, thanks for never getting in the way of what God called me to do. Thank you for allowing me to serve others even when I may suck at times with serving you at home. Through ups and downs, through good and bad you've remained consistent. I'm so very thankful to God that he blessed me with a Proverbs 31 angel like you. I honor you and I love you! Alaina, daddy's baby, thank you for sharing me with the entire world. You are so special and chosen by God. His hand is on your life and you inspire me to do what I do daily. I love you babe! To my older children Alexis and Isaac IV, you two have grown to be awesome young adults. I have so much more to learn about fatherhood and everyday I'm asking God to make me better. My trial and error has cost me a lot, but I won't ever stop working on getting better! Thank you for your patience, I love you guys with all my heart.

To my mom, for being the very first example of what serving looked like, you are my SHERO! For every time you were taken advantage of, over worked, under paid but it never stopped you or hindered you from your assignment, thank you. God couldn't have given me a better living example of love than you. I love you! To my sisters Angie and Kim, we in some shape, form or fashion share this same story because of the way we were raised. I thank you guys for always being honest with me and treating me like a brother. Never impressed by my gift, you guys have always loved me for me. That means the world to me. I love you both.

To my closest friend and team of 1 from day 1, Chidonna, thank you for your constant sacrifice to me, my dreams, my vision and my goals. You probably take more from me than any one person can handle. Yes, we fuss and fight, but you have served me and my vision with the ultimate grace. When I said no, you said yes, when I said I couldn't, you said you can and you will. Thank you for pushing me into this uncomfortable place of favor. I love you! To my brother & road manager Kevin King, thank you for believing in me and supporting me without envy or jealousy. You get on my ever-loving nerves, but I wouldn't trade u for the world. I'm grateful for u brother.

To my Pastor and spiritual father, Bishop William Murphy, III, you came into my life just in the nick of time. You're the only Pastor I've ever had that cared more about my soul than my gift. You cared more about what you could give to me versus what you could get from me. I honor and love you sir! Pastor D, you are so sweet, consistent and confident, which is a rare combination in a Pastor and First Lady. Thank you for being you and I love you.

To my sister, best friend and bossy mother Tasha Cobbs Leonard, you have been a breath of fresh air in my life! Without a shadow of a doubt, God placed you in my life to help save my life! I'm a fan of your gift, but I'm more impressed with your life! Thank you for never biting your tongue when it comes to me, whether I liked it or not! Thank you for speaking into my life and confirming the word of the Lord on countless occasions. I love and honor you! Kenny Leonard, thank you man for the consistency and encouragement you give me constantly. The way I've watched you serve others down through the years has been a blessing to me and I honor you for that Bro. I love you!

To my best friend and brother James Fortune! Man, I could write another book about you LOL, but thank you for always encouraging me! You have been a true friend indeed, and I love u and I'm proud of your resilience. We're just getting started! To my extended family and friends, I can't begin to name you all and I don't have enough space, but I'm so thankful and grateful for your love, support, prayers and words of encouragement. Thank you and I love you all.

To my church family, The dReam Center Church of Atlanta, we're not just a church, we're a family! Period. And lastly, I want to thank everyone I've ever served, or served with from Pastor John P. Kee, Men of Standard, Bishop Hezekiah Walker, Donald Lawrence, Kirk Franklin, Pastor Tye Tribbett, Fred Hammond, Yolanda Adams, Bishop Marvin Sapp, Isreal Houghton, Donnie McClurkin, Mary Mary, Klarkent, Diddy, Tim McGraw, Faith Hill, every Pastor, leader, colleague and singer. There is something I've learned from each and every one of you that I will forever hold dear to my heart. I too dedicate this book to you. For me, It's not about knowing it all, it's more about sharing what you've learned to help someone else hurdle what you went through. So, thank you for coming on this journey of SERVICE, My Words. My Life. My Truth.

TABLE OF CONTENTS
& CHAPTER GUIDE

SERVICE

MY WORDS. MY LIFE. MY TRUTH.

FOREWORD
BY TASHA COBBS LEONARD

The definition of what servanthood is can be located in the life that Isaac Carree leads. Isaac and I share a very close bond with one another. Through our friendship of 5 years and counting, I have witnessed incessant servitude in action by watching him. He is not just someone who merely serves, but he serves with passion, faithfulness, and without selfish ambitions. He serves with his hands and his heart, giving every task the very best he has to offer. He freely gives his time and efforts to uphold and further the visions of others, and does it in the spirit of serving others the way he would serve himself or expect to be served by others. And the most admirable thing about it? He does it all with joy and gladness.

The current trail that Isaac has been blessed to blaze is proof that servanthood is still the precursor to greatness and the hinges that the door of success swings on. It's evidence that before your own dreams and visions can prosper, you must find yourself aiding in the prosperity of someone else's dreams and visions. Before stepping into a solo career, you would find Isaac selflessly standing behind the dreams and visions of others. From singing background vocals for giants in the gospel music industry such as Kirk Franklin and John. P. Kee to serving and supporting his local church, his hands were always diligently at work. And even with now having his own career, dreams, visions, and goals, servanthood is still strong at the core of everything that he sets out to do. If there was ever a time "service" needed a spokesperson, Isaac Carree, without question, would be a worthy candidate.

There is one principle that I will always push and promote to the world: sonship. I cling to a firm belief that, when we lend our lives to helping someone else carry what God has entrusted to their hands, we place ourselves in the best posture for God to widely open the doors to our own dreams and visions. The objective of service is never about the doors that will open for us because of what we do for others, but open doors, is indeed the favor we receive for being found service. God has an outstanding track record of lavishing an abundance of grace on lives that are built on helping others.

From firsthand experience, I can vouch for the power of servanthood. I have seen the reward of being honorable and lending a hand to lift others; and for that reason alone, I will always challenge others to assume a posture of being a servant. In a world and time where the majority seems to desire nothing more than to be seen, I believe the most honorable way to be seen is to be seen serving. This incredible book penned by my brother and friend, *Service: My Words. My Life. My Truth.*, so eloquently highlights the power and purpose of the posture of servanthood. As you navigate the pages of this book, I admonish you to grab hold of the jewels you will find. If you do so, there is no doubt that you will be inspired, challenged to become better, and strengthened in your call to carry the cross of service.

Tasha Cobbs Leonard
Grammy Award Winning Gospel Singer

INTRODUCTION
BY BISHOP WILLIAM MURPHY, III

If you keep reading, and govern your life by the principles that are shared in this book of master keys, your life is about to change for the better. I can say this with confidence because of the old adage, "When we know better we do better." If you keep reading, and then commit to govern your life by the principles that are shared in this book of master keys, life as you know it, will never be the same.

Service: My Words. My Life. My Truth., is going to provide you with an extremely transparent look, into the ascension of one of our nation's most prominent voices in gospel music, and in culture. Isaac has made his story, our story, and given us an inside look into what it truly takes to become a living legend.

I can remember some 20 years ago, when I first encountered "Men of Standard", and I was in awe of the vocal prowess, and the humility, as they didn't know me, but immediately embraced me, as a brother. Who would've thought that 20 years later, I'd be serving Isaac and his family, as their pastor? I'm blown away at God's Mind, and how He strategically plants people in our lives, to help us grow, and mature.

I've been the benefactor of Isaac's ministry for over 2 decades, and watching him serve, and shift, into this new place, has been a real blessing to behold. The scripture is clear, "And if you have not been faithful in the use of that which is another's, who will give you that which is your own?" (Luke 16:12), and this book of master keys, is going to provide you with the examples, and the encouragement you need, to qualify for "your own".

"Serving" is a lost art, as type of forgotten science, that qualifies the servant leader for something bigger and better. Serving is the master key, to a man's ability to make his or her dReams become their reality. So thank God for Isaac's "Yes", and for his willingness to share his words, his life, and his truth.

If you keep reading, and govern your life by the principles, and master keys, that he shares in this manual for the Millennial Christian, I promise you, your life will never be the same! I pray that as you apply these same principles, that you will find yourself walking in the #SameGRACE, that has made our friend, and our brother, and one of our favorite people, a living legend.

We thank God, for *Service: My Words. My Life. My Truth.*

William Murphy, Lead Pastor
The dReam Center Church of Atlanta

PREFACE
FROM A SERVANTS HEART

For twenty-eight years of my professional music career I have been in a position of serving. It just came natural to me, it never bothered me, I never felt less than, I never felt left out, or felt like I was missing out on anything because I was serving. I enjoyed being of service to everyone I served. In the process of serving, I always asked questions and I always paid attention to details. Why you ask? I had no idea at the time, but in hindsight it all was for this time and this purpose. Who knew that with the cards that were dealt to me, that this would be the hand that I would have to play.

God has an amazing sense of humor. I remember hearing these words in my spirit, "You're a good leader, but if you ever want to be a great leader, follow and serve someone great". The greatest reward that I've ever received as a result of serving is that God never forgot me, even when people did, He honored every sacrifice.

We can easily fall into a place of craving the approval of people because we somehow have made ourselves believe people can promote us, but God's approval is all we ever need and should want. The bible says in Luke 10:2, "the harvest is plentiful, but the laborers are few". In other words, everybody wants to shine, but no one wants to buff. I made up my mind a long time ago to never lose my dreams, goals, and passion while serving, but never force them on the people I'm serving.

The most popular question that people ask me is, "what would you say to an up and coming artist who's trying to get into the business"? My answer is never what they really want to hear, I can tell by the expression on their faces. I always say, "Matthew 6:33 says, seek ye first the kingdom of God and His righteousness, and all these things shall be added unto you". Then, I say "always find yourself serving someone"! I'm not writing this book trying to impress you, I'm writing this book because I really believe that my journey can help fuel someone else. If Jesus can serve, then who are we not to?

Mark 10:45 teaches us that "For even the Son of Man came not to be served but to serve, and to give his life as a ransom for many". In Philippians, Paul uses a different form of the word for servant here and the fact is that almost in every place where the word servant is used in the New Testament it is the Greek word doulos, which means a slave, bondman, man of servile condition. Jesus had all glory with the Father in heaven yet emptied Himself of His glory and took the form of a servant. Even though He is equally God, He didn't count it as something to grasp or hold on to, but for our sake, He gave His life.

It's sometimes hard to serve because you must be willing to put yourself last. It's a war between flesh and spirit. Paul had apostolic authority, yet very infrequently did he use it. Paul became a "bond servant" (doulos or slave) for Jesus' sake. Paul, having the great commission from Jesus Christ did not proclaim himself but Jesus Christ as Lord and humbled himself in the sense that he too was a servant for Jesus' sake. If Paul saw himself as a servant to Christ, how much more should everyday believers see themselves as the same, a servant for the Great Master and Lord, Jesus Christ. Mark 9:35 states, "And he sat down and called the twelve. And he said to them, "If anyone would be first, he must be last of all and servant of all."

We live in a day and time where everybody wants to be a leader, but no one wants to serve! There have been millions of books written about leadership but very few books written about servanthood. You do realize Jesus measured greatness in terms of service, not status! God measures your greatness based on how many people you serve; not how many people serve you. The more we push our agenda the less we'll accomplish, but the more we serve the more God will give to us. The disciples argued about who deserved the most prominent position, and 2,000 years later, people still jockey for position and prominence. Even Christians want to be "servant- leaders" not just plain servants. But to be like Jesus is to be a servant. Now please understand anybody can serve but that doesn't make you a servant. What makes you a servant is your heart!

I never miss an opportunity to serve, because I know God honors it and ultimately, I want to please him. One of my greatest joys has been watching other people's visions, goals, and dreams come to life and knowing I played a part, all because I was willing to be unselfish and be a servant. God has employed me and empowered me to share with the world what it took for me to get where I am and what it will take to keep me here and take me even further. I can't stand to be around someone that says they're a servant with a nasty disposition. You're not doing me any favors. You should be doing this unto the Lord. But that's why a lot of people are chasing jobs, positions, titles and career opportunities. They think their gift is enough. Your gift will get you in the room, but your character will keep you there.

Serving is also putting your vision and dreams on hold to help undergird someone else's. If serving is below you, then leadership is beyond you. David's first trip to the palace was not as king, his first trip to the palace was as a servant! We must learn to serve our way to the top. It is with that mandate that we must posture ourselves in service. We are commanded to serve God. Jesus was unmistakable. Matthew 20:28 says, "Your attitude must be like my own, for I, the Messiah, did not come to be served, but to serve, and give my life"

SERVING 101

THE MAKING OF A SERVANT

SERVING 101
THE MAKING OF A SERVANT

Greensboro North Carolina in the seventies and eighties was a place for dreamers. With not much to do besides school and church, as a young man, I had my own dreams of being a pro basketball player. I spent much of my time on the court. There, nothing else mattered. I was always athletic and when you're tall and lanky like I was, basketball was the go-to sport. While I didn't recognize it as discipline then, I showed up to play every day, determined to be the next Michael Jordan. I was good, in my mind. Basketball was my way out. It was going to make me rich. I had replayed it over and over in my head. I was going to be a basketball star.

If I wasn't on the court with my friends, I was begrudgingly being dragged around to what felt like every church in the city. My mother was a musician for our church. In fact, she was a lot more than a musician, she was the choir director, minister of music and keyboardist for several Greensboro churches. Sundays didn't belong to me or the basketball court, they belong to my mom. With my two sisters in tow, we would travel from church to church and from service to service every week for my entire childhood. While it wasn't basketball, it filled our time and was the launching pad for the character built in each one of my siblings and the foundation of this book that birthed the servant in me.

I was a silly kid. Tall and awkward I'm sure but it never bothered me. My sisters shared a room in our home, and I my room was at the end of the hallway. My feet would always hang off the bed and peep through the covers. I wasn't a morning person, but as I stated, Sunday mornings didn't belong to me. For me, this meant church. Rolling out of bed on Sunday mornings meant that there was not much room for the anxieties of the day ahead nor the restlessness of the night before. The goal for me was quite simple, it was to beat my sisters to the bathroom, so I could be fly for the day.

Just down the hall from my mother's room, she could hear and see through the walls putting abrupt stops to any morning sibling bathroom fusses. That lady could scare you with a stare. Sunday mornings was loud. My mom would wake us up banging on our bedroom doors saying, "Rise and Shine. Give God the Glory". There would be music playing in the background and she'd be singing and praising as she prepared for her day. Fluffing hair, spraying perfume and me adjusting her girdle, as she hummed a song or hymn. Like a prayer chant that finishes the prayer or a reverb, she would hum a song that steadied us as we prepared for the day.

The drive to church may have only been 7 to 10 minutes away. Greensboro is a small city, you could literally get from one side of town to the other in 15 minutes. Every day we piled in my mom's brown and yellow Ford Pinto station wagon. It had to be the ugliest car known to man. It had the woodgrain on the outside and everything. My sisters and I would pile into that thing and it got us from point A to point B. That's the first car that I remember us having.

Pulling in the parking lot, my Sunday morning memories of gravel roaring under the wheels, the cracking of the heavy wooden doors of the church and the smell of peppermints and strong ushers perfume. I knew that I was in for a long day. Church on Sundays felt like it lasted an eternity. We had Sunday School from nine until eleven. The choir would march in immediately after Sunday School ended. My mom sat on the organ. Once morning devotion with the choir members ended, she was ready for service. Strong in statue, with the sweetest eyes that alluded to a humble strength. It was like she was magic. From the start of the day, to the end of the day, I heard her voice singing, watched her lend a helping hand, travel from location to location, teaching, ministering, serving with grace, gratitude and dedication.

Church ended at three o'clock. Some Sundays we would go downstairs to the church's basement to have dinner. We'd be sitting in service drooling over the smell coming through the vents of the church mothers cooking greens, fried chicken and fish, mac and cheese and all the fixings. Most of the times, we would go to my grandmother's house for Sunday dinner. She was old school and would start cooking her dinner the night before.

Theoretically, it would have been great to be greeted with a warm meal after a long day of church. Unfortunately, we would still have to wait another hour for the cornbread to be finished. For the life of me, I could never understand why she wouldn't just start making it an hour before we got there. We had YPWW (Young People Willing Workers) service for youth from six to eight and then evening service until ten. So, we'd have to go back to church on a full stomach.

Those moments would create a foundation that would shape my perspective about servanthood. Without a single complaint, I watched my mother serve a community of people. I'm sure there were moments in her journey when she wanted to complain and quit but she didn't. Watching my mom, Sunday after Sunday, week after week was my first introduction to servanthood.

Ambition is the sort of thing that exists without a plan, but I believe it is fueled by the desire to have better and be better. The desire, in a young man from Greensboro, NC born to a single mother is what I would dream about. It was the desire to win. I'd lay awake at night thinking about who I wanted to be, and what I would become and most importantly for me as a young man child, how my life would change and who I would be able to take care of and provide for once all my dreams and ambitions became a reality. I had seen success. I watched it every day on TV. I knew people with nice cars and nice homes. I wanted it for myself, and for my family.

As a young boy, my ambitions were limited. As I grew older, so did my desire to leave the south. I wanted to see the world and become the great man I was destined to be. What I did not know but would soon learn, was that there would be many sacrifices and trials that I would have to overcome. There would be many times ahead when I would lose it all. I knew I would be a winner, I just had no idea what it would cost me. There would be times ahead when I'd insist that quitting was the only way to see relief. I knew that I was willing to do what it would take and I had the courage and the strength to do what needed to be done. What I didn't know was the cost. I had no idea that the cost would be much more than ambition alone.

When I was a kid, they used scare tactics to teach us about God. We would be afraid to leave before the benediction because we might get in a car wreck. I would try to fit in at school. Everyone knew me as a church boy. So, I struggled to prove them wrong. I knew who God was but out of fear. My mom was strict. No school dances, no parties, no secular music. I adapted to the culture that I was a part of. Everyone around me was a part of that world, so the tactics didn't seem odd. I've been in church all my life, but I didn't develop a relationship with God until I left home. My mother was so positive. She wouldn't let things shake her. She would focus on the solutions VS the problems. Those principles would keep me as I would start my own journey. As a parent, I understand that it is less important to teach your kids to be hostile and demanding in unfair situations and more important to teach them how to operate in love and humility.

UNDERSTANDING SERVING

Most people have good intentions and have specific ideas about how they will live up to their dreams and achieve their goals. We set big sights on finishing school, or landing that job, or buying a new house and starting that business. If you're anything like me, a large part of what motivates you is to reach a level of success where you can create a better situation for yourself and the people you love. We are constantly pushing ourselves to do better and be better. The pursuit and drive to always level up means that along the journey, it will be necessary to learn from someone else who has been where you're trying to go.

In our digital age, with information being accessible to anyone with the internet, one would assume that it would be easier to just take a webinar or watch a YouTube tutorial about how to map out your success plan. Unfortunately, there are so many lessons, experiences and character building projects that you just can't learn from the other side of the screen. These lessons must be learned by getting your feet wet and hands dirty. The world of academia and business for example, understands this concept with the internship process that requires students or employees to have experience doing the work that they've studied. Preparation has proven to exceed the benefits of studying alone. This is essentially why serving is important to us as Christians.

The very thing that made Christ famous, is the same thing that makes us Christians, that is the commitment to serve others. To be in service to God means to be obedient to His commandments. When we serve customers, a team or an employee's needs in business, we are providing them with a good or service. Serving means to perform a particular function or to assist and help for any given reason over a period of time. Our reasons to serve as followers of Christ, is because of obedience and love. Whether it was from the example of my mom, working and serving in ministry, or through the hard lessons that I've had to learn in life, I knew that serving would lead me to the success that I'd imagined for myself. I understood that if I wanted to be the best and impact lives all around the world that I had better submit myself under someone else who was already doing the work.

There are many components to serving, as its complex definition explains. Changing form when used as different parts of speech, assisting, helping, providing, caring and fulfilling are all Christian principles and are all characteristics of Christ. Serving is essentially the act of being like Christ. This gives us a competitive advantage when measuring up to our opponents. Because of the grace that covers us and the favor of God that surrounds us, we will always go farther as a result of serving.

We should serve with a purpose to please God first, and as a resource to our own personal agendas, last. There is absolutely nothing wrong with the way the world approaches serving. It pleases God when we all stretch ourselves to learn something new. He loves when we grow, especially when our success benefits the needs of someone else. I believe that God always honors and covers us when we use our gifts in service of others. In fact, the very gifts and talents that we each uniquely possess, were gifted to us by Him to be used to edify His kingdom. "As each has received a gift, use it to serve one another, as good stewards of God's varied grace: whoever speaks, as one who speaks oracles of God; whoever serves, as one who serves by the strength that God supplies—in order that in everything God may be glorified through Jesus Christ. To him belong glory and dominion forever and ever. Amen" (1 Pet. 4:10–11).

The bible teaches us that God not only honors us with grace, but He also equips us with the power, strength and authority when we operate on His behalf. To me, this means that I started off as a winner. It means that my gifts and talents are really His gifts and talents. It means they are already at level best. Serving gives me the advantage of having my gifts nurtured and explored, sometimes revealing new dimensions of His gifts working in me.

THE BENEFITS OF SERVING

WHY WE SERVE

THE BENEFITS OF SERVING
WITNESS TO MIRACLES

There are many benefits to serving other than gaining experience alone. With over 28 years of tutelage and service to some of the music industry's top selling artists, experience is the obvious thing that I've gained. However, there were so many things that I've seen and witnessed. From my vantage point, so much of what I've seen is the manifestations of God's promises and miracles up close and personal. The thing about successful people and the successful people I've served with, is that they are all walking in their purposes. They are all magnets for miracles and I got to see them demonstrated. I witnessed the power of God open doors and make dreams come true. Because our talents are gifts from God, I've watched Him be glorified on stages around the world.

One of the most remarkable miracles performed by Jesus was at the Wedding of Cana. He was a guest at a wedding along with his mother, and a few of the most famous servants, the disciples. During the festivities, Mary informs Jesus that they'd run out of wine. It is the servants who Jesus asked to fill the pots with water. "Jesus said to them, "Fill the waterpots with water." So they filled them up to the brim. And He said to them, "Draw some out now and take it to the headwaiter." So, they took it to him. When the headwaiter tasted the water which had become wine, and did not know where it came from (but the servants who had drawn the water knew)," (John 2:7- 9). What would have happened if the servants had not been in their places? Would we have an account of this miracle? This would be the first of many miracles that Jesus would perform, but it was the role of the servants, that manifested the miracle of Jesus turning water to wine. When we serve, we are the ones who witness the miracles as they are happening. We are the ones getting the first dose of the power of God.

RESIDUAL BLESSINGS

When serving, you're not only a witness to miracles but you're in position to receive the residual blessings. Have you ever been the recipient of hand me downs that seemed like they were custom made for you? It's like a sibling or family member gifting you something that didn't necessarily suit them but it was exactly what you needed and what you'd been looking for. God sees you when you're serving.

In fact, I believe that when we serve, we are most present with Him. It is those periods that He is walking with you and talking to you and orchestrating experiences just to teach you. When you're serving, God is performing miracles and working things out in your favor. He is placing your face in front of people and on platforms that introduce you before they expose you. I've always believed that when I'm serving, He's stretching me and showing me just how far I can go.

GROWING YOUR SPIRITUAL GIFTS

This is important to so many of us who are serving in ministry. We may be asked to serve in a capacity that we may not see as a fit. That is because we can't see what God sees. Whether you're a singer, musician, preacher or hospitality worker, know that your labor is not in vain. As you give your time and your service, it is important to look at the work that you're doing from this perspective. If God is requiring me to greet people, He may be stretching my temperament to handle crowds of fans for the moment when I'm at the center of the stage. If you're asked to work in administration or in some organizational aspect of the church, then perhaps God may be preparing you to launch a business. He could be giving you the workload and challenges now that will help you navigate your own personal brand later. Knowing that while I am perfecting my craft, that God has a strategy and knows the exact formula for my success. It helps me remember that all things are working together for my good. I am reminded that even when the season seems drab and dim and in the moments when I may have felt like I wasn't doing enough or wasn't producing enough, God was building me.

THE HEART OF CHRIST

I couldn't imagine where my life would be today if I hadn't learned early on how to serve the needs of others. In fact, serving helps me to be more Christ-like. It helps me to mimic the heart of Christ in my day to day life. I find myself making a conscious effort to be more kind throughout the day.

I intentionally have come in to the practice of expressing gratitude and verbally telling people thank you. This is because of the posture that I've mimicked as a result of serving. I am always learning to have more compassion towards people. Serving ignites a fire in me to give more and just to take a little extra time to care for someone, even if it's just in passing. I am often reminded of the scripture that says, "and let us consider how to stimulate one another to love and good deeds, not forsaking our own assembling   together, as is the habit of some, but encouraging one another; and all the more as you see the day drawing near" (Hebrew 10:24-25).

Serving helps us to see people like Jesus does, rather than how we'd like to see them or judge them. I've learned to exercise a little more grace, whether it be when I'm stressed out driving in traffic or I'm exhausted from work and have to complete my hunny-do-list. The peaceful posture that I've learned through serving others, involves a lot of heavy deep breaths, but it causes me to pause and not to react to every little thing. Serving allows the Holy Spirit into my life and into my heart. Serving has taught me how to chasten my tongue and watch my mouth and what I say.

When you're serving other people, especially in ministry, you learn and become conditioned to not be quick to inject your opinion or emotion in every situation. I've learned how to let things play out and be more patient. In the many things that motivate me and inspire me to serve, pleasing God is at the top of that list.

It's so much easier to navigate life when you don't focus on the work. I always tell people to focus on the reason and purpose behind the work. For me, I'm pushing to build a legacy for my family. I am working and serving to learn as much as I can learn and to gain the tools and insight that I'll need as I continue to grow my career and platform. Most importantly, I'm serving to please my father. When I focus on those things, and not on the sometimes mundane tasks at hand, then I can present my gifts and service with the disposition of joy.

PATIENCE & FAITH

It's only natural, that when we're right in the middle of something, that we can't always see the end. It's not always easy to be in a situation where you're waiting on God to do something in your life but you're still required to show up and serve. I have been in situations when I've been waiting on a miracle to happen for me at home, while I was on the road serving. Managing what my eyes see and directing them to ignore the natural reflex to panic, is never easy. There is a grace that I've learned to focus on when I'm in tough situations.

When I'm serving, I've learned how to activate Ephesians 3:20 "Now to Him who is able to do far more abundantly beyond all that we ask or think, according to the power that works within us". I've learned how to just give Him all my stuff. After years of God showing me over, and over again, how He is covering my stuff even the stuff that hasn't even surfaced yet, I know that He's busy redirecting all sorts of stuff and hand delivering a few of those exceedingly and abundantly blessings. So that when I return, things are better than I left them.

THE SERVANT
WHO WE ARE

THE SERVANT
THE SERVANT SINNER

It's easy to look at the many ways that we serve on a day-to- day basis and get overwhelmed. Most of us have to manage our job, our husband or wife, our extended family, our church, health, finances and children. In some way, we serve each of those entities and sometimes more throughout our week. All needing your attention and your hand on it just to make it function. Your kids need you for food and shelter and transportation and everything in between. Our jobs, sometimes require overtime or extra hours for special projects. Sometimes, we can find ourselves being stretched in so many different ways all at the same time.

There have been instances when I've served everyone else and had to come home to serve my family or my church. I have to serve them with the same tenacity that I've served in with everything else. I should serve my family with the same enthusiasm that I've served my boss, or my pastor or my hobby. I have to serve them with the understanding of what my time with them means to them. Remember, I am not serving with my gifts. I'm serving with God's gifts. This means that God has ordained me to serve the people in my life because he has given me a gift that they specifically need to fulfill their purpose. If I don't guard the gifts that He has given to me, then I'm saying to Him that I can't handle more. How could He continue to give me more people to serve, if I can't handle the ones who are already assigned to me.

What about the things that God has required from us that we didn't ask for. Do we still have to treat those assignments with the same regard that we treat the things that we want to do? Of course, we do. There are so many questions that I've asked myself as it relates to my purpose to serve others. I would often ask God, "why me?". I'm a sinner after all. I haven't always made the best decisions and I don't always get it right. I'd ask God, "why me?", especially as it related to serving in church. I always assumed that God wanted me to be perfect. I assumed that if anyone found out that the very things that were being ministered about from the pulpit, are the very things that I was secretly struggling with. Then I realized that God was using me, because I was just like the sinner. I was the sinner. God showed me that He is simultaneously fixing us all. Sometimes He uses the broken to draw more brokenness. He needs them to see some of their stuff in me and me to see me in them. Those lessons remind us that God still loves us and is using our stuff, to spread doses of His love and light to the world.

This doesn't mean that serving the church doesn't require you to be more responsible and committed. You are expected to be a leader and to practice walking and talking and living like Christ. Because God insists on using sinners like you and me, He only requires our heart. He already knows all of your stuff. He still chose you. He's already seen what you're going to do about that situation in your life that you know you need to stay away from. He knows you're not going to always make the right choices and has still chosen to use you. God was using me when I was in the middle of some mess, and He continues to even today. It's such a wonderful and comforting thing to know that God still wants to use us anyway.

As a singer, I've served in both secular and Christian environments. I've seen how God continues to use so many people that the church would consider sinners. It's made me realize that it has never been God who has disqualified us from the rewards of His grace through service. It's usually our own rhetoric that makes us focus on the things that separate us and restrict us from reaching our full potential. Sometimes we can be so afraid that our stuff will be exposed that we don't realize that through serving He is trying to expose your stuff to the covering of His grace. I wrote "Clean This House" because I literally needed God to do that in me, from the inside out. I let my stuff be exposed in the words of that song and of all of the songs that I've written, that one landed on the top of the charts. If I wasn't a hot mess, I would never have written that song. It was my prayer.

God has used the stuff or the mess of many people to serve His kingdom. My boy David was the tiniest thing. He was the smallest of all his brothers. He was the youngest and not in line to be King. David's mess was his size and his lack of strength. He was just a shepherd boy. He wasn't concerned with whether or not fighting Goliath would make him look weaker and expose his mess.

He was only focused on the task at hand and that was to fight the massive Goliath and free his people. Focusing on the purpose, David then used his mess to develop a strategy. All he needed to do was avoid the pitfalls of his size and focus on how he could use them to trick the enemy. In his weakness, little David had developed a strength. He learned how to evaluate his opponent not by size alone. He recognized that the fully armored Goliath is going to move slower because of the weight of the iron. He also recognized that Goliath is blind and his strategy was to get close enough to Goliath to propel a devastating blow but far enough away from the weighed down giant to miss any retaliating attack.

This is how we should deal with our mess. We need to focus less on our weaknesses being exposed and focus more on serving through it. Because of David's mess or perceived disadvantages, God used him to set his people free and covered him the entire time. What a promise of victory we all have, to be cloaked in sin and still be used by God. What Goliath is God preparing for you to defeat? How will your mess help you to build and enhance God's kingdom? There is something in your mess that has qualified you for what God has next for you. In being obedient and serving with the heart of God, as we pursue excellence, we must allow God to perfect us through the process. We must create an environment that is free from the negative dialog of doubt, and allow God to manifest His glory, not only in us but through us.

THE UNDERQUALIFIED

Oh, the joys of having your boss or leader pull you in to serve in a new area, potentially with more responsibility and more visibility. There may be other people in your department or ministry who may have been there longer or who may be more qualified to perform the task. Instead of choosing them, your leader saw something in you that they believe could benefit the project or organization. As our ministries and businesses grow to embrace changes in the economy, in commerce and to enhance digital performance, there are specific skills and services needed to fit the scope of work ahead. It is in the organization's pursuit of progress and growth that we often see these changes in talent.

Many of us serving in these roles, have been faced with public opposition, negative team morale, self-doubt and have so many questions surrounding a shift in assignments. How do we handle these situations? How do we navigate our new roles with both gratitude and authority? How do we serve in roles where we feel we're not worthy and may be under qualified? How do we still dominate with authority and confidence? We do so with the assurance that God has chosen us because we possess what He needs to share his love and light around us and to position us for what's next.

Some of us have been out of a classroom or training environment for so long that we've forgot how this goes. When in a classroom setting, and the teacher calls you to the front of the class to demonstrate a math problem, he or she usually already knows if you know the answer. The purpose for you to demonstrate the problem in front of the class is either for you to demonstrate to them, how to solve the problem or it's designed to help you. Your public demonstration could show you how not to get stuck. Most of us usually struggle at the same point in the problem. The instructor knows this, and has pulled you out to help you get through it, so you can move on to the next thing. Your position at the chalkboard or the head of the class, is still in a learning capacity. You are really still just there to learn.

We are not always expected to know everything in the positions we serve in. Just know that God is either using you to help someone else, or He's using the platform or the assignment to teach you something. The platform doesn't necessarily insinuate some type of hierarchy in readiness. Sometimes, not being called to serve in a certain capacity could be because it may be a lesson that you've already mastered,

God could be saying that you're already ready. This is important for us to remember so that we don't be so swift to take on the role of offense. Many times, what may feel like rejection, is actually a compliment. I've seen this in my home church with my pastor. I've watched him assign people to serve in expanses just because as a pastor, he had the wisdom to see that they may need to grow in that area. He also knows his sheep and he can see in the spirit realm what we can't always see in the natural.

He uses all sorts of people to do all sorts of things and because of that, I've watched his ministry flourish. I watch how he keeps a watchful eye over those serving in ministry, creating opportunities for people to grow in so many areas of their lives. Because of his leadership and how he enables people to serve in areas that can grow the kingdom, even outside of the walls of the church. I've seen businesses begin out of talents and gifts that members may have discovered while serving.

There is nothing that we can do to separate us from the love of God (Romans 8:39). In fact, God needs your stuff. When we focus on how we thought God would use us and when we thought that we would be ready, then we miss the miracle that He could be trying to show us as we serve through our stuff. What if President Barak Obama thought that he couldn't serve the country as president because he wasn't a white man? What if he felt like America wasn't ready for a black president? He could have used many things to disqualify himself from even attempting to serve the country as president. The odds were stacked up against him. Obama is not only black, but he has Hawaiian and African origins, a Muslim name, he smoked pot, inhaled and is one of 12 United States presidents who had not served in a military branch. That sounds like a lot of reasons to not serve to me. But we all know how that story played out. We all know that Barak Obama was the 44th President of The United States of America who served despite all the things that could've disqualified him. Twice.

There are so many phenomenal singers out there. There is nothing that qualifies me to serve with the likes of Kirk Franklin, John P. Kee,

Men of Standard, Diddy and Tim and Faith. Let me be clear, there is nothing extraordinary that I had to offer, but everything that put me in the positions to serve those ministries, has been because of what God saw in me. He is what matters. It is my prayer that we be delivered from the narratives of doubt, fear and rejection. I pray that we begin to really embrace the power and love of God as He waits with open arms for us to say yes to serving and building the Kingdom of God.

WE'VE GOT TO DO IT

Our lives are consumed with so much stuff, well at least I know that mine is. I've got the same sorts of busyness that fills up my day as you do. In fact, when I'm not busy doing the stuff that takes up so much of my time, I'm busy thinking about them. When I'm resting, I'm building a to do list, following up with my team, promoting, building and developing the things that are on my long list of stuff to do. The thing that makes me say yes, is that I get that serving makes us all better people and that our service to others is ultimately a reflection of God. All that rhetoric sounds good, but where do we find the time? How do we serve the needs of others or our community outside of the things that we must do?

I found time to serve when I realized it was the key to my destiny! When I realized that was another way that God would prosper me, to give of myself as He gives to us all. I found pleasure in helping undergird someone else's dreams, goals, and vision. And I literally began to see the hand of God open door after door for me the more I served. It wasn't my voice, nor my personality that set me up for success, it was my service! So I ask, how can you NOT find the time to serve? Well, I would highly suggest that you get out of your own way and make the time knowing that it ultimately honors God, and then he'll give you the desires of your heart!

I remember a time during the Christmas holiday season a few years ago when my mind was so fixated on Christmas shopping. I was so busy and had so much to do. Suddenly I got a random call from a friend asking me to volunteer some time at a local nursing home. I was like "huh"? I really didn't have the time. I was so overwhelmed with my agenda, but it was a great opportunity to serve and give back to someone else. So I agreed to do it, but I put stipulations on how much I would do so that I could still have time to do what I wanted, which was finish my Christmas shopping. Well, once I got there and saw all those beautiful people excited to hear me sing and spend time with them, my stipulations went straight out the door! I ended up singing so much that they almost had to put me out! So what I'm saying is this, don't get so caught up with yourself that you can't fulfill the needs of others! Make time to serve others, because what you make happen for someone else, God will make happen for you!

THE COST

THE BLESSINGS IN SACRIFICE

THE COST
THE BLESSINGS IN THE SACRIFICE

As spiritual people, we understand that along with the hard work, training, dedication and faith that is required to complete our goals, also comes a certain level of sacrifices. Most successful people have sacrificed something to get where they are today. They've had to endure some things and go through some uncomfortable situations. I've made many sacrifices throughout my career. I've paid the price of being in uncomfortable situations because of what I had not yet learned about navigating the industry. Today, my biggest sacrifice is being away from my family and friends, for sometimes long periods of time. As a young entertainer, the sacrifices looked a bit differently.

When I was a teenager, I didn't know anything about the music industry. I had an opportunity to sing with a popular gospel artist. The first year was cool. I was a young man from Greensboro, traveling to places like LA, Vegas, Detroit and Chicago, meeting people I'd seen on television. Parts of me felt like I had made it. The other side of the story was that I wasn't making any money. I found myself in a situation where I was working, but I couldn't exactly afford to live. I couldn't pay any of my own bills. I was eating because someone else was feeding me. There were times when I ate because someone threw a bag of cheeseburgers to the back of the tour bus a couple of times a day. That was considered craft services. I'm talking about feeding grown, hungry adults two double cheeseburgers a day.

I can remember the day that it really hit me. It was about nine adults living in a two-bedroom apartment in Charlotte, North Carolina, without money or food. One day while we were cleaning and sorting clothes, we found a twenty-dollar bill crumpled up in the pocket of an old pair of jeans. We were excited and relieved because we could get something to eat, but a silent fury was building inside of me. I was usually hopeful and optimistic, but this time I was mad. You can exist without a lot of material things, but a man without food is an angry man.

That twenty-dollar bill came just in time. We went down to the convenience store that was in walking distance of the apartment building. I can remember it being a very hot day. We were sticky, funky, I'm sure uncomfortable and hungry. That day, we were able to feed eight to nine people with that one twenty-dollar bill. It was in that moment, while I was angry and completely frustrated, that I also recognized that those sacrifices were necessary for that time and that assignment. I stayed because the assignment had not ended. I stayed in that situation because I knew that God would honor my sacrifices. Parts of me may have wanted to quit, but I believed in the purpose and I stuck it out because of that.

I had learned a valuable lesson by the time that assignment had ended. Being hungry is not a cost of servanthood, but when you're just starting out and lack the experience to handle your business properly, then things like that can happen. It was a learning experience for me.

Today, I'm never in a situation where I'm hungry. I'll never not be able to eat. That's probably why I'm so greedy and take eating so seriously now. I mean, when I eat, each meal is a production. I'm always thinking of what to eat because my mind is still working through the psychological trauma caused by being hungry. That was the first time that I had experienced poverty. When you're serving, there may be times when you're uncomfortable. The best way to stay encouraged is to never lose sight of the fact that you're serving the purpose and not the person.

I knew that while I may have been temporarily uncomfortable, that I was serving a greater purpose. The artist that I was serving was ministering to people and touching lives all over the world, and I was a part of that. I was serving a purpose. It's important to understand that everything is not about how you feel. It's easy to get tired and become discouraged, especially when it looks like you're not being appreciated or the sacrifices aren't fair. I say to you, stay the course. Serve in love. There are some lessons that you can learn without sacrificing comfort in such an extreme way as being hungry. Pay attention to people around you, perfect your craft and always stay positive. "For God is not unrighteous to forget your work and labor of love, which you have showed toward his name, in that you have ministered to the saints, and do minister" (Hebrews 6:10). The absolute most valuable lessons that I've learned from the costs of serving, are the knowledge and an understanding of how things work. I've experienced both the positive and negative aspects of serving. When we pay for things, we're honestly only expecting or anticipating the positive results of the product or service. We never want to find ourselves in the percentage of error as it relates to performance or quality. If I buy some J's, I expect a certain quality. I don't expect for my shoes to represent the two percent margin of error in production quality. There were people who didn't do business right, people who didn't pay me, but it taught me to do my best anyway, because God would honor that. I learned how to take negatives and make them positive.

What I received for the price I paid was access to information that only experience and wisdom could teach. I've gained the ability to be able to adjust in uncomfortable environments. I paid the price and I received a toughening of the skin. I got calluses. Today, I can stand and walk through anything because my heels and feet are callused. My hands are callused. I won't get burned easily. It means that no matter what situation that I am put in, I have gained the wisdom that allows me to see beyond how uncomfortable things might be in that moment. These experiences in fact, are constant restorers of my faith. They serve as a reminder of the grace and love that God continues to cover me with when I'm serving. Knowledge and experience are worth the price you'll pay. There's truth to the adage, "knowledge is power". Because of what I learned in these streets, I can achieve anything.

THE SERVANT'S SACRIFICE

As a singer, I've spent much of my time on the road traveling, doing tours and shows in many genres of music. Because of that, I am around lots of different types of people, often in small settings and for long periods of time. I'm usually the person who's clowning in the room and find myself the unintentional life of the party. I love creating atmospheres where I can have fun. When you're on the road and you're missing friends and family day in and day out, it can be tough to serve and stay positive. I like to try to create an atmosphere where people are comfortable enough to be themselves. So, naturally, I become the silly person. I believe that when people are laughing, they are more relaxed and more likely to be themselves. So, I like to laugh, after all, my name means laughter. I become the light in the room. It also means that at times when I'm off or having a bad day, people notice.

The older I've gotten, the less I want to be gone from home for long periods of time. It's like I'm itching to get back. It's hard at times but I'm sure it's what I've been called to do. One day when I was on the road last year, I got some bad news about my mom. I couldn't break and I couldn't be angry, I still had to serve. I had to give of myself when I was scared, when I was angry and worried. I had to pour my heart out on stage. Historically, some of the most challenging situations in my life have happened to me while I was out of town, serving on the road.

I don't think it's fair to put more weight on people when they are on their jobs, being paid to do their level best. It creates an impossible work environment and bad energy and bad morale is contagious. When I got the bad news, I couldn't go home at the time. I couldn't just shut down and deal with the myriad of emotions that I was feeling. I had to somehow gather myself, and complete my assignment.

For entertainers, so many things can affect our performance and our energy on stage. For me, it's no different. What ends up happening, is that when the lights go off and the show is over, your favorite entertainers are so stressed and depleted that they are one step away from a crisis. There is extreme internal stress that exists from having to bottle it all up to get through a work day, while smiling, and being fly, and being funny, all while singing with perfect pitch. When artists are on the road, we are forced to deal with all types of challenges alone and away from family and friends.

You may be serving your local church or ministry. You may be working in an industry, where it's your job to serve the needs of others. The late-night meetings and all-night practices and missed birthdays and even vacations, all are a part of the price we pay as servants. What I've gained is how to find balance. When I'm serving others, I've learned how to come out of my own stuff quickly. There are so many things that exist in the worry zone, or in the judgement zone, or in the hopelessness zone of stress.

I've learned to find release in serving, and let whatever heaviness I may be feeling in my spirit, be free on the stage. Now, I almost look forward to serving when I'm stressed. I have learned that there's a purging that happens when I selflessly serve the greater needs of others. There is a replenishing grace in that space.

Serving is not singing background for someone who is paying me. Serving is catering to the needs of people, adding light and love to their journey. I like to approach people in love. I try to not make my issues other people's issues. This posture prepares me for ministry. It is the compass to embodying the personality of a servant. When I'm serving, I try to be in a good headspace, surrounded by good energy and good people. So, wherever I am, if it's not fun, then I would probably be miserable. I'm usually thinking that if I'm having a hard time being away from home, missing family, events and especially my bed, then so is everyone else around me. I am always conscious about making sure the energy is light, fun and positive.

What I do is people. What I know about people is that they are not always operating at one hundred percent every day. They are mostly doing the best that they can with the perspective and circumstances that they are given. People sometimes show up to work carrying the weight of their bills, relationships, family issues, self-doubt, hopelessness and even depression. With everything that serving has cost me, and the lessons that I've learned along the way, I've been able to engage with people in a way that I may not have on my own.

I've gone on stage several times heavy. At times I've felt like maybe God didn't appreciate that. I felt like He wanted me to come as my best self and not distracted by things around me. Through true relationship with God, I've learned that He values our vulnerable, open hearted service in ministry. Through the experiences that I've had while serving, I have been able to write and sing songs that were initially about me, but end up helping so many people. God shows us His glory in so many ways. Serving keeps my heart open to see that. God loves broken people because He is the ultimate potter. He does His best work when you're broken. I know this to be true because there are broken pieces in us all. I've had fans and people to come up to me and tell me that 'Clean This House' changed their lives. What they didn't know is that it changed mine as well. It was a prayer, a cry out, a song of broken pieces that was used to heal and deliver people. God used my brokenness to mend so many others.

I've had some amazing testimonies about how my music has changed people's lives and I'm so grateful. I'm humbled to know that because I served, someone's life changed. I understand the weight of my assignment. I want my music to help people to realize that they are not alone, and remind them that God has not forgotten about them. When I was at my lowest place or discouraged about the industry, people's testimonies have literally pushed me to keep going. I've had someone to tell me that playing 'But God' on repeat kept her from committing suicide.

Or that 'In The Middle', changed my life. Someone once told me that they were on drugs and in an abusive relationship and they were impacted by a song that I wrote when I was down and searching for hope. There are many sacrifices in serving, but there are even bigger rewards when you persevere. Those testimonies push me. Those testimonies make the cost worthwhile. It humbles me and pushes me to serve better. So today, when I'm serving and I get tired, or weary, I keep going, because God's plan is always bigger than mine and that my sacrifices today, will not only benefit me in the end, but could potentially save someone's life.

A SERVANT'S HEART

I want to share the truth about what it means to operate with a servant's heart. I want to impart in you that the wisdom and favor that you'll benefit from because of your service. Whatever it is that you want, whether you're spiritual or not, will come because of what is in your heart. At our core, should be love and compassion and the willingness to serve the needs of someone other than ourselves. There is an abounding grace that exists in that space, and it always comes from serving. With everything that we want, with every tangible and intangible thing that we set our hopes on, there is a cost, there is a price that must be paid. Every millionaire and successful person will tell you about sacrifices they made along the way. Even the birthing process comes with pain and sacrifice. I say, see it through. Stick it out. "And let us not be weary in well doing: for in due season we shall reap, if we faint not" (Galatians 6:9).

Unfortunately, being a good person doesn't make it any easier to serve. It doesn't eliminate obstacles and it certainly doesn't entitle you to any type of reciprocal service. When we think about being a servant, most people think about some sort of slave. I believe that serving, means to carry the torch of hope, to cater to the needs of others and to bring light and love everywhere to everyone.

When our hearts are tilted towards God, our service should be a reflection of His love and an extension of His grace. I am certain that I am more equipped to succeed because of the lessons that I've learned while serving. It's not that I know everything, but I'm more experienced. I'm putting what I have gained and learned all on the table. I've been fed fluff all my career and I've had to ween through that with a strainer, sifting through all the junk. Time is so valuable. I wish that someone had shown me some of the things about serving that I've had to learn the hard way. Time is one of the most important things that we can't get back. I hope that the time that it took me to absorb some of these lessons, could help people save years of time wasted on dead situations. In serving, I gained a strong aptitude for growth.

It's been twenty-eight years since I started my career and I'm still learning and growing. I'd like to share insight and truth about what it takes to get what you want and how to serve your way to achieving your goals. I want to be very clear about the reciprocal action of giving and receiving. This message is universal. It's not just about ministry and it's not just about the music industry. It's more about the flow of the world.

There is no output without the proper input. Serving transcends religious, social and economic parameters. There's a special covering in serving. What we think is that the blessing in serving exists because the person or entity you're serving can get you "experience or access", but that's not the case at all. There will always be favor in serving others. The grace and favor sometimes manifests itself by protecting you and keeping your gifts from being exposed while you're still developing them.

You have got to know enough information to be able to succeed when it is your turn. I learned so much of what not to do and what to do better during my time serving other people. When it was my turn, I was able to come to the table with my gifts in a pure, raw and authentic way. I was able to write a chart-topping song that was really just my personal prayer. A servant's heart, serves not just your desire to succeed, but it serves the heart of the people. When people are your priority, your love is shown in service.

PRIDE VS
OBEDIENCE
A LESSON IN FAITH

PRIDE VS OBEDIENCE
OBEDIENCE TAKES FAITH

One of the earliest lessons we learn in life is the importance of being obedient. Our paths to the road to obedience may be different, but they all yield the same results. Some of us learn the practice of obedience through the testimonies and experiences of others and some of us learn after we've experienced the consequences of disobedience. Obedience is a large component of serving. To be obedient means to be compliant with an order, request, law or submission to another's authority. A large part of our role as servants is to do what we're asked, under the authority of our leader.

Ultimately, we as Christians are commanded to be obedient to our leaders as well as God. There are times when what we are required to do may not make sense or even seem fair. There are instances when being obedient to even our leaders can take an act of faith. In many ways, obedience is a reflection of our personal faith. Faith is such a large conduit in our decisions because being obedient can sometimes mean that we have to trust in something that we can't see.

We have to be obedient in faith, knowing that we only have a limited view of what is to come. When you exercise your faith in obedience, your actions say that you understand the bigger vision and are doing the work that it takes to get there. I am called to too many things not to be obedient. There have been times in my life when I could only see the bigger picture because what was in front of me didn't reflect the things that God had promised me. There were many more instances, when my obedience was a result of the activation of blind faith.

I was presented with an opportunity to work in the secular world, which I wasn't quite sure about. I knew that it would be a good business decision, but I was a bit reluctant to accept the booking because the church can be ruthless. If they feel you've betrayed them or that you're not loyal to them they will rip you to pieces on social media. I took the decision to my accountability team. This is what I call my team of people who serve with me and no matter what, they'll tell me the truth about anything and everything. They are people who I care about and most importantly, I value their opinions. After talking to my pastor, my wife and some of my close friends to get their take on this opportunity, they all confirmed what God had said to me in my spirit. I accepted the booking and as expected, I got ripped for it. The church folk even talked about it on their blogs saying, "Chart Topping Gospel Artist Isaac Carree is on tour with Diddy".

The Bad Boy reunion tour took place in 2016 and after prayer and spiritual counsel, my community scolded me because they didn't understand my assignment. I was sure that God told me to do this, so I knew that my obedience would cover me. I obeyed even amid scrutiny, naysayers, critics and people who didn't even know me. I did twenty-eight years of only gospel music and took one secular gig and they beat me up about it. I remained obedient despite their harsh criticisms.

It was to date, the greatest experience of my life. I learned more in those three to four months between rehearsals and touring than I learned in my entire career as a gospel artist. As a community, the church in general has done so much to separate itself from what they deem to be bad, that they've missed so many things. Often, our business as artists fails because of our limited knowledge. Our interaction with the rest of the world, limits our perspective on people, current events and just life outside of our own reality. I saw more, experienced more and I gained relationships that opened new doors for new opportunities. My obedience in that situation allowed me to be able to offer my community, people who may not have ever been able to experience certain things, exposure to talent and people they would have never met. Experiences like the Bad Boy tour have allowed me the opportunity to create events like my conference, 'The Plug' where I can share wisdom and insight about the music industry based on my experiences. Had I not gone, I would be one dimensional. I would have been yet another singer with one perspective recycling the same songs.

It's a culture where everybody is trying to get in where they fit in. The mentality of exclusivity in churchy people in many cases, causes our impact on the world to be limited. Sometimes the things that God has uniquely called us to do is outside of where we're comfortable and what's familiar. You can't be a global brand with the perspective or point of view that doesn't extend past the church pew. In other words, you can't reach the world with a store front mentality. So, I understand what God has called me to be and do.

I understand that there may be things that are required of me, that may cost a great deal of temporary anguish. In understanding that, while I say yes and serve, I know that God is moving things around for me. I know that I'll need the unique set of skills and experiences that I gained over the years, to navigate success and longevity. As a servant, you must understand that assignments are not forever. You can serve forever, but you may not be on that specific assignment forever. Every assignment brings about a new opportunity, so you should be obedient to God, despite what it looks like.

I came back from the Bad Boy Tour refueled and energized. I saw things I'd never seen and experienced things on another level. For the first time, I was able to look back at what I had been a part of for 28 years and see that it's not what it's cracked up to be. I'm not talking about perfection, I'm simply talking about the way we judge people because they don't look like us or do it like us. We treat the church and Christianity like it's an elite country club. We're judgmental, we have nasty attitudes and we're quick to send everybody to hell. That doesn't line up with the word of God. Jeremiah 31:3 says "Yea I have loved thee with an everlasting love therefore with lovingkindness have I drawn thee". Then we wonder why people don't subscribe to our agendas or want to come to our churches.

I was convicted. I was able to look back and check my heart. Now I exercise grace more and I'm so much more sensitive to the perspectives of other people because of my experience working outside of my genre. I could cross the fence and look back and see what I was a part of. At one point, I was like you, these jokers are flawed.

The church looks really messed up from other people's perspective. That's why this generation doesn't come to church, that's why they don't fool with us or subscribe to our agenda. I was like, wow. Just look at what our posture is. In the church, we can be so rude. Why would anybody want to be around that?

Being obedient in that situation taught me a very valuable lesson. It stretched my perspective and points of view. When church people found out, some of them said to me, "I get it, go be light in darkness". I get the analogy that they were trying to use. But who says that they are dark and we are light? In many instances, serving in the secular world made me realize just how dark the church really is. I could never align myself with that statement before I took that gig. Yes, I am a gospel artist who was serving one of the biggest brands in hip hop and no, there is nothing about me that makes me light and them darkness. In fact, most of the "worldly" people that church folk talk about, live better lives than the people in the church. Why does it have to be darkness?

I think as Christians sometimes, we think that because no one knows what we do, we're somehow qualified to talk about people and what we know that they do. I would rather be around people who smoke weed and do this and that, at least I know what I'm getting. The truth is that it's always easier to serve truth than it is to serve a lie. Jesus rocked with all sorts of people. The moral compass that the world holds people accountable to, as a servant and as a person, emphasizes that character is the most important quality. I learned the importance of developing an individual code of conduct, no matter what genre because that is what a servant does. Despite any personal prejudices, the Bad Boy Reunion Tour taught me that the same place of love that serves in ministry, is the same source of love that should fuel the way we treat one another.

Most church folk, come from a long line of church folk. It's a good thing in many cases, but in the ways that we deal with the rest of the world, our perspective is not only skewed by what we've learned in the church, but by what we have been taught for generations. We have created our own rules about church and what to do and what qualifies us for God's love. Somewhere along the line, we have adopted a culture where we ostracize and exclude anyone who doesn't do Christianity in the same way that we do. I know many gospel artists who live just like the rest of the world, or worse. Shoot, I know my life. I know the things that I've done. There are people outside of the church who are responsible adults with families and careers who give back to their communities and live more wholesome lives than many of the people I've encountered or served with in church. So, who's to say that because of the perception that we try to show in public, that we're light. We can publicly confess and profess to be whatever we want, but if we're foul privately, we are actually dark and deceitful. I do not subscribe to the us and them narrative. I can't seem to align myself with the concept of me being light and them being darkness. It's judgment even in making that declaration. If we are going to really impact the world, we have to serve each other from a place of love.

Today's church culture thrives on the worldly practice of the little man serving the bigger man. Often, it muzzles zeal and excludes people who want to serve. We have successfully perpetuated the slave and master role. It doesn't always happen, but there are so many cases of abuse of power in the church. As servants, we should be careful of this.

The key is knowing who you are and if at any time you are serving someone or somewhere and you are dealing with emotional, verbal or physical abuse, it's time to leave. With an influx of movements like Black Lives Matter, Black Girls Rock, the empowerment of women and the support for black men, the church at times still preaches empowerment but exhibits quite the opposite. It's position on servanthood and even the matriculation of leadership is something that we've gotten wrong for so many years. If you're serving and growing weary or impatient, remember that God always makes the increase. I've never looked for anyone else to exalt me. It's difficult at times to see it while you're in the middle of it, but God is in control, and when it's your time, all things have already been aligned to strategically work towards giving you the desires of your heart.

Serving in ministry and working for someone both have obstacles. You have to create the standard. When you serve someone, you are expected to be loyal to them. This does not necessarily mean that you have to align yourself with everything they represent or that they're attached to. Serving means understanding the difference between walking with someone through their stuff and condoning it. I mean the ugly stuff, like affairs, and scandals and false accusations.

When you're serving, you are literally working towards carrying out someone else's purpose. Just like your stuff that never stopped the grace of God in your life, neither does the stuff in their life. You are often around people's families; their spouses and you are also often a witness to some very personal things about your boss or leader. This access is a privilege. When you serve, you have a front row seat to watch how God moves. We serve as an example of God's love. This is why it's important that you never forget about your why, the assignment. You are there to perform a job. You are there to perform a service that they might need to fulfill their purpose on this earth. You are there, even in the smallest role, as a part of something bigger. Your voice, your smile, your warmth, your ability to excel at your job can be the difference between the success of the next icon or president or even the greatest artist of all time.

You may not be able to stand in the front of the stage with the lights shining on you and you may not have millions of Instagram followers, but you can absolutely have whatever you are committed to work for. More importantly, you can have whatever you are willing to wait for.

WHEN PRIDE WINS

There is a sacrifice that you'll have to pay as a result of being disobedient. It may not seem like a big deal now, but it's much easier to just be obedient than it is to deal with the fallout of not. Obeying always works out in Christ. If God says go, then you've got to trust Him and go. Even when the situation may look horrible, as a servant of Christ, we have to hold on to what the bible says, that our paths are ordered by God. We sometimes insert our own thoughts over what God is saying. From a natural perspective, of course we think that we know what would be best for our lives. Instead of really trusting the spirit of God we lean in to our own understanding of things, sometimes making a mess of them. The thing that we don't know and can't see is what He sees and what He has prepared for us just on the other side of this lesson.

I understand that the sacrifice could mean that I could lose everything, just because I wasn't obedient to one thing. For me and the things that I desire, I am not willing to sacrifice them because of the temporary discomfort that obedience can sometimes carry. When God calls us to do something, it sets the foundation of what He can trust us with in the future. "Whosoever hears these sayings of mine and does them, I will liken him unto a wise man, that built his house upon a rock" (Matthew 7:24). I knew early on that the dreams and goals that I had for my life would require a strong foundation. The lessons that I've learned in obedience and the journey to get there is what keeps me solid today. Even when everything around me pushes me from every direction, I am solid because I am obedient.

Pride can be a tricky thing. We want to operate with honor and with dignity for ourselves and our families because we represent Christ. There are other characteristics of pride however, that can cause trouble. I can imagine the pride that Abraham felt. He was a proud father and loved his son Isaac. He was a man of faith and knew that Isaac was a gift from God. In fact, God had promised Abraham that he would give him a son, so Isaac was a promise fulfilled.

When God told Abraham to offer Isaac as a sacrifice, he had more reasons not to be obedient than most of us have ever had. But he did it anyway. I can imagine that he questioned God. I'm sure he was even angry with him. What if pride had won. We know what God had in store for Abraham, but he couldn't see it at that time. We know that God would not require him to complete the sacrificial offering of his son, but Abraham didn't know that. He obeyed God despite what he felt and saw.

Obedience has benefited me in many ways. I remember when Kirk Franklin first called to ask me to go on the road and sing with him. At that time, I was still with Men of Standard and was headed down a different path in my career. I had done the group thing and the choir thing, and I felt like that's not the path that I wanted to take anymore. I was ready to be a solo artist and take the world by force. I heard God tell me so clearly to do it. I had people in my corner saying, "why would you do that? Why would you go backwards"? But I heard God say, that if you want to be a good leader then keep doing what you're doing, but if you want to be great, then you've got to submit yourself and study and sit with a leader who is going where you want to go. You've got to submit yourself and serve.

I knew that my assignment was greater than what I could see. I understood that there would be some very valuable lessons that I would be able to learn throughout the journey that would shape me to be a better artist, entertainer and person. My act of obedience to sing with Kirk took me places and has given me a platform that I may never have had.

God was teaching me through that period of obedience. He was grooming me for my destiny. In serving, I've learned the importance of obedience as it relates to your next assignment. Your next level of success is directly connected to your ability to be obedient while in your current situation. Obedience is essentially the place of grace. At the cross section of new and next, lies obedience. It's like a fork in the road and depending on your decision, the result can cause a lifetime of stress or a platform filled with purpose.

Today, I seek God with every decision in my life, large or small. Not because I'm afraid or can't make decisions on my own, but because of love. God loves us in a way that covers our faults and supports our dreams. "The man who says, 'I know him,' but does not do what he commands is a liar…. But if anyone obeys his word, God's love is truly made complete in him" (1 John 2:4-5).

THE ABUSE OF
SERVANTS
UNDERSTANDING ABUSIVE LEADERS

THE ABUSE OF SERVANTS
UNDERSTANDING ABUSIVE LEADERS

It's a very common term, "church hurt". We hear it all the time, usually when someone is explaining why they don't go to church anymore. This is of course at no direct fault of the church. It speaks to the misuse of a system designed to teach serving that at times, has been, mismanaged. Most Christians who have served in ministry for any period of time, have experienced hurt as a result of the conduct of their leader or co-laborers in ministry. I've been in situations where serving has pushed me away from God, rather than bring me closer. It can be a very difficult situation to manage, when you are on an assignment and quitting isn't an option. Despite your personal decisions to serve, others don't always make it easy. In fact, some leaders abuse their servants by treating them like slaves. So, what do you do in those situations? How do you handle a leader who requires too much, or who is rude and disrespectful?

After you've heard from God and made the commitment to serve, the last thing you expect to encounter is an ungrateful and abusive leader. With everything that I do to make sure that serving is a priority, the last thing I want to feel is unappreciated. Sometimes I'm surprised at how I'm able to do all the things that I do in a day, but without mapping out time to serve others, everything else that I'm trying to do will suffer. I revel in the space of grace and covering that I've received through serving. Rude and manipulative leaders are not what I have time for. I've encountered a few and they definitely made it hard to be obedient and to stay on course.

In trying to understand how to deal with an abusive leader, I had to like any other victim of abuse, first accept that it was happening. The signs aren't always easy to identify, especially when its coming from someone you respect and admire. They usually differ based on the personality of the leader. There are some very common traits of abuse in leadership that we should all be aware of.

THE ULTIMATE AUTHORITY

Abusive leaders regard themselves as the ultimate authority. In ministry, this is easy to identify because God is the ultimate leader. In business and professional environments, abusive leaders may be defensive and rarely take advice or opinions from anyone other than themselves. They believe that they are the smartest, wisest and most relevant. They subscribe to systems of hierarchy and act is if the universe revolves around them. The abusive leader is not compassionate, and love is secondary to personal agendas for profit and advancement. A true leader is a servant. While they may not serve someone else in the same way that they serve you, they serve something greater. They recognize that they are not the ultimate authority and will encourage you to serve in other areas, and not just them.

LOVES AUDIENCES

Who loves a good crowd? You guessed it, an abusive leader. In situations of conflict, for example, the abusive leader will insist on exercising their power and handling issues in public. Whether through public shame or embarrassment or complete disassociation, the abusive leader will choose to resolve matters with an audience. They may even discuss issues and disagreements with others, rallying for support from a crowd. If you ever find yourself in a disagreement with an abusive leader, they'll be sure to involve other people who will see things as they do.

MANIPULATION AT ITS FINEST

Manipulative leaders always find a way to remind you what a wonderful opportunity it is to serve them. At any sign of hesitation to do what they ask, abusive leaders will try to convince you to be obedient to what they say by questioning your loyalty and threatening your job security. The abusive leader will also try to use guilt to push you in to obedience. They will often overlook things that you do well in order to find your areas of weakness to use against you later. This sort of leader will try to create an environment where they convince you that you owe them. They'll use their authority to dictate what you can or can't do based on what they've done for you. When an abusive leader does not get the response that they want from you, they use many things to try to manipulate you. From money, to politics, to the future of your career, the manipulative leader will do just about anything to convince you to do things their way.

SELF-GRATIFICATION

The abusive leader is one who is addicted to self-gratification. Their ego requires titles, position and power to feed it. The tasks and assignments are solely based on fulfilling the fantasy of obtaining ultimate power and authority. In essence, they seek world domination, even if it's through the internet. They create a larger than life persona and require the people serving them to support this fantasy. It's easy to recognize this type of leader because they are highly driven by material things and make it a point to show them off. They place the importance of objects before compassion and serving people. They won't serve you, but you'll serve their narcissistic orders that are often unnecessary and don't teach lessons of servanthood, rather they perpetuate the role of slavery. These leaders don't care about the people who serve them, in fact, they enjoy the idea of having a slave. They treat the people who serve them as if they are less than or as if they don't deserve the same kind of grace and favor. Their selfishness and self-centered behavior is often at the detriment of someone else.

CONTROL FREAKS

Controlling behavior lends itself to much more than abusive leaders. We all know people who display this behavior. They like to have things go a certain way and they never trust anyone else to get things done. This is the opposite of leadership. The role of a leader is to give guidance and instruction to help an individual or a group to learn an important lesson or achieve a specific goal. The controlling leader is a dictator. They will refrain from teaching their servants because they believe that they are the only ones who can do things right. They will be micromanagers who believe that the only way to get something done, is by doing it their way. While the root of many badly-behaved leaders is insecurity, they mainly operate in fear. Their goal is to create predictable and routine environments. To do this, they try to eliminate creative thinkers and any type of innovation that is outside of what they've created. Abusive leaders fear failure more than anything. It's not so much that they are driven by success, their motivation is not failing. This causes them to want to duplicate the same formula for success in every aspect of organizational operations. They prefer robotic obedience.

BAD COMMUNICATORS

When a leader communicates well with their team, at various stages during the job or assignment, the servant learns to perform the duties of their jobs more effectively and efficiently. Understanding the scope of work, the specific tasks involved, and the leaders preferred method of performance, all need to be communicated effectively. An abusive leader is often a poor communicator. They give minimal instruction to avoid being clear. If the leader communicates clearly, any errors, mistakes or bad judgment calls would reflect their authority. Without giving clear instructions, the leader can blame any negative responses or judgement on the people who serve them. This behavior is not only abusive to those who serve them, but it can be oppressive and narcissistic.

WHY DO WE ALLOW ABUSIVE BEHAVIOR?

I've served many versions of the abusive leader. My commitment to my assignment often blinded me to their tactics. I'd think, maybe if I just do it their way, then they'll be happy. I would try to go out of my way to prove my loyalty when they questioned it. I would sacrifice time and money, when they felt like I wasn't committed enough. I'd focus on all the things that they had ever done for me and let that be the reason why I served. It wasn't until I took a step back that I recognized that I was serving an abusive leader. So, what do you do next? Once you've realized that the person or businesses that you've committed to serve, is taken advantage of you, then you've got to move on. We allow abusive behavior mainly because most people have a tough time recognizing abuse. There are so many things that generally protect us from abusive treatment in the workplace. Ministry, however, is the perfect breeding ground for abusive people to thrive in. This is due to the single leader with multiple servant design. Whether in the workplace, in personal relationships or when working in ministry, many people have a challenging time leaving toxic situations, even once they've identified symptoms of abuse. This is because our culture has been socialized to believe that there is a certain sort of strengthening that comes from an abusive leader. The general idea is that tough rulers are just strong rulers and that people need to be forced into doing the right thing. The same concept is evident when parents spank children, or when we wage war on another country.

Many abusive leaders are full of charisma and charm. They have very likeable personalities and people usually enjoy being around them. They show loyalty or favor towards people long enough to gain their trust and respect before abusing them. I once served in a capacity where my leader was so cool, that I would miss some of the rude things that he would say about other people. Over time, the things he'd say about other people became the same things that he said about me. I overlooked some of his negative behavior because I had grown to respect him. As servants, we agree to accept their behavior as a trade-off to their greatness.

We all understand the basic principle of compassion. Whether it be through religious values or just in the practice of being a good person, we generally try to be compassionate to each other and express forgiveness. Especially as it relates to our ministry leaders, we tend to be too forgiving of their abusive actions. It's as if we automatically associate rude behavior with the stress of leadership, so we let things slide that we shouldn't. It is why we don't question what they do, and why we don't hold them to the same standards as our peers. In the workplace, human resource departments and other external organizations provide a safe place for workers to address some of these concerns. But what happens when you're serving in ministry or serving with an organization or cause? How do you handle abusive leaders when serving in environments where there's a greater cause other than profit? This can be hard to do.

We must find a way to confront those authority figures. Maybe, in the same ways that we would in the workplace, in private settings, with someone else present as a witness. The best way to handle leaders in social and religious environments is with compassion and empathy. There is usually an overwhelming feeling of fear as it relates to any fallout from conflict. This is especially when the fallout is a result of objections to their leadership style.

Most of us don't want to be perceived as the difficult one to work with. No one wants to be the only person who speaks up and potentially be outcast or blackballed. I once served with a leader who was abusive in the most manipulative way. Every time I would address something with him, he insisted that I should be a better team player. He would always try to convince me that I should be grateful for the opportunity to serve and that being obedient to him would be honoring God. I didn't see it at the time, he was being manipulative. He was well connected and would also insinuate that he would connect me with people and expose me to his network, and for that I should be grateful. I didn't want to make an enemy with the wrong person, so I stayed longer. I endured the abusive behavior longer than necessary.

In general, I tend to be a very understanding person. I am loyal and faithful because honestly, it's what comes most natural to me. My personality coddles the bad and sometimes abusive behaviors because while I tell people the truth, I also try not to judge them. I try not to let their temper, bad mood, or aggressive behavior shown a few times, determine my commitment to the assignment. It is important that we find balance. When we serve people in leadership, there are times that we see things about our leaders that we may not like. It may not always be abusive to others but could just be of questionable character and integrity. Here is one of the best things that I've learned.

Those things may overlap in the way that they lead and interact with people. Often, serving a leader means that we have a vantage point that allows us to see the way they lead from a unique perspective. We can tell if their abusive behavior is their character or if those unfavorable behaviors are temperamental responses. What I cannot control is how the person I'm serving handles their assignment to lead, but what I can do is remain obedient and operate with integrity at all times.

In ministry, we understand that we accept serving as an assignment. We commit to giving our time, talent and service towards spreading the light and love of Jesus Christ. This makes it harder to leave a relationship that is abusive. Nobody wants to be considered a quitter, or worse, an opportunity hopper. It doesn't have to be difficult, however. We should use the same measures of grace and compassion that we would expect for ourselves. We should hold our leaders accountable and challenge them to work collectively towards the goal. We should be more devoted to the purpose of ministry than to the people we serve in ministry with.

Serving can become such a big part of who we are that it can be a part of how we identify ourselves. I once had a colleague who served a national non-profit organization for over a decade. She was a chairman and had served on several committees throughout her tenure in the organization. Like many of the people who worked and volunteered for the organization, she had become a part of its fabric and it became a part of her identity. She was no longer, Jane Doe, she was Jane Doe of this national organization. Her family grew up serving alongside of her and helped to perform the functions of her position. When the season ended, she had a hard time separating who she was as an individual with who she was as a part of the organization.

When we are truly committed to something, we never really realize how much of our time it actually takes. It's not until a holiday, or when someone else points it out to us, when we realize how much time we're planning and how much time we're actually serving. When we overexert ourselves and over-commit ourselves to the many tasks it takes to serve in ministry or in a non-profit, we reciprocate abusive behavior from the leader to ourselves. Self-care and balance are both important when we evaluate how we handle serving, especially when you're serving in abusive environments with overzealous and aggressive leaders.

While we are to put God first, even in serving the church, we are also responsible to hold each other accountable, including our leaders. Managing our leaders is not much different than managing any other relationship in our lives. If we tolerate abuse, usually it will persist. It's important to remember that it is our responsibility to teach people how to treat us, and that includes our leaders.

Because abusive leaders not only affect one individual but the entire team, it's important that we change the culture around the way we handle abusive leadership in ministry as well as in the workforce. Team morale, productivity and effectiveness can all be affected when a leader is abusive. The conflict between a leader and the people who serve them usually will result in conflicts between team members who need to work together fluidly to perform the tasks at hand. Both the workplace and ministry are environments where people from diverse backgrounds, serve in social environments where the leader sets the standard and everyone else follows suit.

When the leader is abusive, speaks badly to people and is disrespectful in any way, it directly demonstrates that type of behavior is acceptable with the organization. Because the culture of the institution is more determined by the overall attitude and values expressed by its workers or employees, it's important that leadership manages morale properly. You ever notice the difference of the personalities when you walk in a high-end grocery chain vs a standard neighborhood grocer? The customer service, thus the customers' experience is more pleasant and welcoming. When a leader is abusive, they dictate the culture of the organization. As individuals, it is ultimately our decision, whether or not to align ourselves with the culture of an organization led by an abusive leader.

A good indicator that it may be time to move on, is if you are not growing and learning. When you get to a point where you feel like you're just serving out of obligation and not from a place of love, then you've probably plateaued in growth. Abusive leaders create hostile environments of fear and conventionality. In healthy environments, the leader is still a servant and they encourage creativity and lead by example. In situations of conflict, servant leaders address issues head-on. They lead by teaching, and they serve alongside of you, for a greater purpose, other than their own agendas.

As Christians, we entrust our leaders to impart vision and purpose into servants. They are assigned to build and unite servants to work collectively towards one goal. The servant leader provides a covering and pushes you into purpose through experiences in serving. Jesus' hope was for His followers to do "greater things" than He had accomplished (John 14:12). Our leaders should be building, teaching and showing us, just as Christ did.

THE
BALANCING
ACT

MANAGING PRIORITIES

THE BALANCING ACT
MANAGING PRIORITIES

Serving looks different at various stages of our lives. When I was a young man, it was easy to stretch myself really thin. I was everywhere, doing everything. It was easier for me to say "yes" to serve because I was a single young man and honestly, I was ready to learn and soak in everything I could. As I got older, with more experiences and more responsibilities, it took a little more finesse to balance my personal life with serving. This was not because my passion for serving others had changed, it was because my life got busy. At times, the people in my life didn't see serving the same way that I did. They thought that I was doing too much. Most people who serve understand exactly what I'm talking about. Your friends and sometimes family members say things like, "what are you doing that for? Why are you always serving? Are you a slave?". These were all opinions that I've had to face and learn to balance.

This same thing affects many people who serve. Finding the right balance between family, marriage, career and children can be a daunting task. The demands that are constantly competing with each other for our time can be draining. Whether you're single, married, serving with a spouse, or serving with your entire family, there will be instances where one or more of your responsibilities will suffer and serving sometimes just complicates your already stretched schedule. Each one of the things that we've committed ourselves to require maintenance and our time and attention.

More than just maintenance, we are responsible for facilitating growth in those areas. Our children, marriages, career and our spiritual lives not only need maintaining, but growing and maturing. How do we do it all, simultaneously? Living out of balance affects our whole person. Our bodies get fatigued, sick and mental exhaustion makes us cognitively slow and our spirits are likely to be vexed and weary. Learning how to create balance is difficult, but so important. Your house can't fall apart, and your marriage can't suffer because you've decided to serve your community or church. Your kids need to eat and be nourished before you feed the homeless person or a leader. But it happens. In committing to do something good, you unintentionally neglect something else. But for those of us who serve in ministry, and if all of the running around, long meetings and outreaches have pulled us further away from God, finding balance is an immediate need.

Symptoms of unbalance usually become more visual over time. When we begin to feel the pressure, is the best time to shift. Abusive rhetoric such as "suck it up" or "don't be weary in well doing" have both enabled us and created a spiraling dysfunctionality in our lives. Rather than ignoring the symptoms, we should be taking a moment to prioritize and reposition activities. Before shutting it all down, keep this in mind. It's probably what you've asked for. If you've asked God for increase in any area of your life, you've got to know that it will be as a result of your increased effort. Serving, is where that increase is being activated. So, be careful when you shift and reposition things. Be careful of responding to growing pains, but be intentional with your heart about making it all work.

It starts with your mouth. If you're constantly saying, "this is too much", then it will be too much. Your confession should be, "I'm built for this, God show me how". You should take on the disposition of strength. Let the discomfort stretch you. When you're serving, you're there for a purpose and your family and career are equally as important. My key to prioritizing is to schedule everything. I don't assume that I'll spend my spare time with my wife, spare time is hard to come by. I intentionally schedule time with my wife and kids. Whether it's just dinner, or time away, you've got to put it in black and white sometimes to see it. Some people are serving in ministries with their family. It is important that you not blend family time with that. Schedule time away from ministry activities to spend doing things they like. A little bit goes a long way. "The Lord will guide you always: he will satisfy your needs in a sun-scorched land and will strengthen your frame. You will be like a well-watered garden, like a spring whose waters never fail" (Isa. 58:11 NIV).

If you are serving a leader who doesn't have balance in their personal lives, there's a great chance that they will fill your schedule full of activities requiring you to split your time. It is important to release yourself to say no sometimes. Other things like limiting social media use when you're with your loved ones, or not responding to emails after hours could help to balance your time. There's a great chance that if you're struggling to balance serving with your life, then other areas of your life are out of sync as well. It doesn't just go for ministry, but your career, your relationship and your family should not be neglected by anything. I know, I know, it's easier to say it than it is to do it, but scheduling is the only way to eliminate that chaos of busyness. This means including time for yourself.

Over-committing usually means your heart is in the right place. For those people serving in ministry especially, you'll need to set boundaries. It's an individual thing. You've got to decide up front how many days you can commit to being there. It's easy to get carried away with so many activities that you end up serving 5 nights per week. You've got to give yourself time to rest and replenish. The bible introduces rest to us with the sabbath, even God rested. Thus, the heavens and the earth were completed in all their vast array. "By the seventh day God had finished the work he had been doing; so, on the seventh day he rested from all his work. Then God blessed the seventh day and made it holy, because on it he rested from all the work of creating that he had done" (Genesis 2:1-3).

God wants us to live a life of balance, making time to be excellent in every aspect of our lives. I believe that he is especially pleased with us when we find time for family, our community and worship. He has called us to be good stewards of our time. There are so many ways we can maximize the time that we do have. Whatever it is that we're doing, it's important to be completely present with that thing. When I'm on the road and I'm working, I'm fully present there. I try to minimize things that could distract me.

Depending on your work environment, it could look different for you. You may need to minimize social media breaks, or extra chatter time with coworkers. Maybe you're spending too much time on social media or browsing blog sites when you should be working.

When you give your full attention to something, you are honoring God with excellence. The same goes for time with family, friends and with God. When you're not at work, minimize the amount of emails you respond to, or work-related calls you take. Setting time to spend with your family and loved ones, can make a few hours seem like a few days rather than just leftovers. Being completely present can help you to complete more tasks at work and create more memories with your loved ones.

How do you say no more, especially as it relates to serving in church? The easiest way I've managed my heart for serving with the realities of my schedule, is to not say yes too soon. Sometimes we are so eager to help, or feel obligated to do it because someone requested you, but the only person who can handle your schedule is you. You have to be the architect of what serving will look like for you. There are some exceptions to the boundaries that you'll create for yourself, but in general, consider everything before you commit to it. When serving an event, consider how much time will be required for planning or fundraising. Consider how much time will be required for set up and break down and how many hours you'll spend commuting between activities. Consider things like, will this require more than just my time, but money. If you're raising kids, sometimes you need to consider if your yes to serve, will mean that you'll miss an important milestone in their life. You'll have to determine what makes the most sense for you. After all, your family is your first ministry.

There are some things that I just simply have to let go of. As much as my heart wants to, I just don't have time to do everything. Once you've made the commitment to serve and its's no longer working for you, its ok to respectfully resign. So many people who serve the church feel like pulling back from ministry related work, is somehow a disappointment to God. This couldn't be further from the truth. God is honored when we are whole and happy. Being spread too thin means that is not very likely that you're operating in excellence with anything.

If you're already serving and your load is heavy, look at the areas that are most neglected. Fix them first. I often do check-ins with my family to see if I need to adjust anything. You've got to be flexible.

As our children get older, their needs change. For me, it meant that I needed to make it home in time for games and recitals. What always has worked may not continue to work. This applies to our spiritual walk as well. I hear from God just fine when I'm working and serving. When I'm busy, I can still hear God. I've learned how to navigate my schedule, but take time to pray and listen to him. Spending time with God fuels me and gases me up with the energy I need to carry on to my next task or activity.

"But seek ye first the kingdom of God, and his righteousness; and all these things shall be added unto you" (Matthew 6:33). There are times when God requires something different from me. In those times, I know how to call my team and tell them, hey, I need a day with God. If I'm shaky spiritually, in my core, then everything might as well be a wrap.

Most people think it takes some type of magic formula to create the perfect balance between serving and the rest of your life. I wouldn't say that I use a formula, but my priorities are God first, then me, family, work, church and then everything else. I understand that after God, I'm the glue that holds it all together. This means that there must be a moment in there for me. I need to be full in order to serve everything else in my life. It's easy for me to get my time in at the gym, on the basketball court or playing my game system. It doesn't have to be deep or heavy. Everyday I'm not going to get a chance to play ball for 2 hours, but I can take a moment and do something that gives me a break. If God is good, and I'm good, I can serve with my whole heart. You must prioritize yourself. If you're sick, then you're no good to your family. If you have a nervous breakdown from stress, you can't possibly function on your job. I want to present my best self, and while there is an undeniable grace that's attached to serving, I have to get my mind right, first.

Prioritizing what's important to you is necessary when you determine your availability to serve. I have no choice but to make it my priority. I am where I am today because of the seeds that were planted when I was serving. It's something I could never stop doing. I don't care how busy I get, or what other sort of opportunities may come, I am committed to serve. From those serving opportunities came so many visons, such as this book. It's where God births every vision that I carry.

As a young man, I started my career in the service of others. Rather than trying to make service work with my life and my schedule, I include it in my plan. I map out my calendar and itinerary to include not only errands, traveling dates and appointments, but service as well. Whether in ministry, the community or any other commitments that I've made, I stand by my word and make it work. It's important to me to do this because what I know for sure, is that the more I serve, the more God will show favor towards me concerning the matters of my heart. This insight made me eager to serve. I said yes often because I recognized that somewhere in each assignment, there would be a fantastic opportunity for me to grow.

For over half of my music career, I've had assignments back to back. This is not always the situation for everyone. I talk to people all the time who tell me that they want to get involved and they want to give back through service, but they just can't find the time. For the average person managing family time, jobs and serving can be overwhelming. Prioritizing serving is essential to my success. I may not have realized it throughout the years, but now it's very clear. There's nothing else that makes more sense about why I've consistently been working for 28 years. The only consistent effort on my end, has been my commitment to serve. As a singer, I work with several artists, and we all know what it's like to struggle and not know where and when your next gig will be. There it is again, another example of how grace covered me. I have to believe that the unwavering grace and favor exemplified in my life is because of the staunch position that I take as a lifetime servant. I knew then and I know now, that serving will take me where I want to be.

For the last two years, I haven't been working on any solo projects. It wasn't even intentional. I didn't decide, hey I'm taking a break from music, so I guess I'll serve. I started serving in my church and then I decided to go back out on the road. Before I realized it, 2 years had gone by. What was happening in the meantime, was that God was grooming me and growing me up. There were some lessons that I needed to learn. God was preparing me for the next season in my life and career. From that season of serving, God has birthed so many things.

Serving has always given me an escape from myself. There were some things that I needed to overcome and serving created a covering for me. I was still able to honor God and work because of the escape that serving gave me. Have you ever gone through something and it caused you to want to take a break and reflect? Well, realistically we can't always do that. We can't always disappear and be a human, when being in the public eye is what provides for our families. God was showing me that there's a reason for that, specifically in my life. During the past few years, I've realized that it's no coincidence that serving has been the apex of my career. God was showing me that my favorite place, the place where he hides me and covers me, was the place that he wanted me to share with the world. God wanted me to share with you the miracles attached to serving.

There are so many questions that I can't answer about what the future holds, but what I can impart in everyone within my reach, is that serving is the catalyst to peace. There are times when our natural understanding and emotions about circumstances will not align with what we know we need to do to persist and keep going. Feelings of disappointment, rejection, anxiety and stress can all create such an uproar in your spirit, that your peace of mind is shattered. For me, serving has been that bridge of peace.

Now, after spending time away, I've been released to do more music. While I never stopped working, I stopped creating to take a moment to sit and hear from God. I'm not sure why more entertainers don't do that. We all go through moments creatively where we need a fresh start and a new sound. In my prayer for God to use me, and to show me what He wanted me to do, I found the answer in serving. Here's the bonus, God not only worked on my music, but He worked on my heart. He stretched my capacity to love and He healed some gaping holes that were living inside me. God was deliberately showing me how to love all kinds of people from all different walks of life. It's why I found myself working and serving in environments outside of the norm. I worked with people and in genres that are outside of what I do and know best. God was giving me direction and showing me that we've got work to do together to heal our world.

I didn't always understand that God had intentionally created in me the ability to be fluid in all sorts of environments. He gave me this innate ability to get along with just about everyone. I didn't always understand that it wasn't about popularity, but that it was a part of my purpose. I had no idea that the same bubbly personality that labelled me a class clown or life of the party, was because He wanted to use me. God was calling me to action. He wanted me to share his love of service and compassion towards one another beyond the walls of the church. I was struggling with compassion and I didn't even realize it. I was challenged not with being compassionate to others, but to myself. I found that while serving had given me a place of covering and tutelage, it was also a place where I could hide. It was where I could ignore the radical and scary things that God was calling me to do. Service, is what God has called me to, and all of us to do, so technically I wasn't being disobedient. I hid out there, as if He couldn't see me.

I had begun to create internal narratives of self-doubt and fear because I wasn't exercising compassion for myself. I judged myself for the mistakes that I made in life. Mostly, I judged myself for being afraid to take more risks and to step out on faith as it relates to my ministry and my career. Little did I know, that the last season of serving that I was in, that I thought I was hiding, but God was teaching me to stop judging myself. He was trying to show me so many other people in my industry who also struggle with self-doubt, but they still pushed. He showed me other artists who found balance in serving God and being creatively relevant and impactful. Because I serve God through singing, He needed me to see other singers who were managing their personal lives, careers while serving in the public while on even larger platforms than I had been on.

I was learning how to be a servant leader. As God began to impart the next steps of my life, I was internally watching God shift my perspective from the servant to the servant leader. When you've served all of your life like I have, there's a fuzzy line between being a humble servant and a difference maker. The places that God was trying to take me to, as a humble servant, I would've never gone. As a world changer and dreamer, walking in my purpose, I should technically be jumping head first in to those uncharted territories. God used the time that I thought I was seeking clarity and hiding away in service, to light a fire in me and set me on a new course. I took the time to dig into some areas that helped me for my next step. The time I spent away from the public was imperative in getting to the other side of this journey, so I could pour in to you.

God may be trying to do the same thing in you. We understand that certain aspects of serving can be difficult. Dealing with abusive leaders, managing our personal lives and even scheduling issues can create challenges in our commitments to serve. Once you've adjusted your posture to serve, or in my case, remained consistent to a lifestyle of serving, then how do we know when God is pushing us to the next place? Amid everything else that usually affects us, how do we recognize when God is holding us back, verses when God is pushing us? How do we clearly hear from God as it relates to what to do next? How do you identify when you need to find balance?

In my life, I liken serving, to fasting and praying. When we're serving, while we may not be fasting or praying constantly, God is speaking. When our hands are open in service to others, they are also opened to receive the outpouring of God's blessings. We are in the physical position to hear from God and to be groomed and sharpened for our next. If you find yourself serving, and you're in a place where you're not hearing from God, it's time to move on. Most people think that because they are working in the background, that God isn't ready to use them yet. They assume that service is mostly about gaining experience anyway. The truth is that serving God is having VIP seats to impartation. It's where He's speaking to you and giving you instructions and dreams and visions about manifesting the desires of your heart. It is the initiation post and the place where He puts in motion all of the things that will work together for you. The bible says that "All things work together for good to them that love God, to them who are the called according to his purpose" (Romans 8:28).

When we're serving, all things are working around us and for us. Therefore, I leap at opportunities to serve. I need a lot of help and have a long way to go, to get where I want to be. I'll get there, as long as I'm serving.

WORKING
AND
SERVING
KNOWING THE DIFFERENCE

WORKING AND SERVING
KNOWING THE DIFFERENCE

I understand that there is not always a clear distinction between working and serving. When we serve, I think about meeting the needs of someone or selflessly contributing to the benefit of someone else. Working is an agreement to perform a specific duty or task with a specific result. It speaks to one's obligation to provide a service. When I first started singing, I didn't get paid for the first 4 years. My attitude has always been, I'm here to serve. I never stopped. As I grew older, God used my faithfulness and opened doors that translated to money. You've got to be diligent and faithful where you are. I don't think service is connected to a job. It can create a job, but it isn't a prerequisite. I know we hear it all the time, but your gift will eventually make room for you. If you're serving and you feel like, if I keep serving, then eventually I'll get paid, that's not serving, that's an unpaid internship. If you are serving in church, your focus should be about the purpose and mission of the ministry. If you're serving in your community, it should be about uniting people. Wherever you find yourself serving, if your end goal is money, then you're looking for an opportunity. I serve because I want to please God. I want to make Him happy. As the head of my household, I want to set the standard of service for my family, just as my mom did for me.

If you feel underappreciated, taken advantage of and are not growing, then you should say no. When you're not growing where you are and it's no longer propelling you to strive for greatness. You have to have faith enough to go. Sometimes we're being stretched and it's important to recognize that, however, sometimes we're being pressed to move to the next level.

I am reminded of a conversation that I was having with a colleague. We were discussing serving in ministry and the constant challenge to know when it's time to stay and when it's time to move on. There are so many situations of misuse and unrealistic expectations in his serving environment. I was explaining to him that in many ways, serving is like a bird and a nest. There's two perspectives when it comes to this. Some birds stay too long, and some birds leave to early. If you leave too early, you could find yourself operating outside of God's will. If you stay to long because of comfort or familiarity, you can block your blessings and miss your season. You can't allow fear to keep you from going to the next level. If you're serving, and you're having a problem differentiating between working and serving, you either need to shift your focus, or it's time to move on.

It's all about timing. When you're in a serving environment, and it's a church setting, monetization is literally a process. However, I don't believe that servanthood is necessary for the process. When I sang with Kirk Franklin, I served his ministry for over 10 years. When it was time to move on, it was hard for me. I wanted to stay because of the relationships that I'd built over the years. I wanted to stay because the people I served with, had become my family. I wasn't ready for that assignment to end, but I knew it was time. I knew that God honored how I served his ministry and was preparing work for me on the other side. I didn't miss a beat when I left but God didn't reveal my next assignment until I was obedient. Leaving is not always a dreadful thing, it wasn't in my situation. I was also serving a leader who knows God, and who understands that seasons change. You've got to be honest with yourself. Sometimes people are itching for work, they are so desperate to get paid that they are willing to go anywhere and do anything to satisfy their own agendas.

I don't think I've ever treated ministry as a job. My mantra about this is "the gospel is free, but ministry costs". If you want the gospel, you can go to church every Sunday morning for free. The day I started getting paid it became a job. The bible says, "the laborer is worthy of its hire". That's how I take care of my family. Ministry and work go hand in hand. I think it's hard for church people to differentiate between ministry and a job. So, let me explain. There's a side that's work and there's a side that's ministry. When we're booking dates, crunching numbers, coordinating travel and doing business, we're not speaking in tongues and laying hands. Why? Because that's business. That's the job. Ministry for me starts when I'm hearing from God in preparation for an album or a concert. Ministry happens because I want to make sure that I'm sensitive to the needs of the people.

The church has communicated the wrong message about service, thus resulting in the abuse and misuse of people's time. Be careful to not make anyone feel guilty for getting paid for doing music ministry. Its technically light weight prostitution. When you understand the nuances of the position and the scope of work involved, then the decision is ultimately yours. I do recognize that this is huge deal, especially for those people working in ministry. The volunteer nature of church, can be confusing. Most people and ministries have a tough time with this one. How do you balance volunteer service, with work that you should be getting paid for? There are people serving in ministries across the world who will never get paid for their contributions. This is because it is our duty as Christians, to build the church and use our talents toward the glory of God. However, you must really seek God on this one. Finding this balance will be an individual quest. The way one person may be able to juggle family life, career and volunteer church work may be vastly different from the next. If you find yourself in a situation where something in your life is suffering because of the amount of time you spend volunteering or serving, something will need to shift.

There is a component of church that must be run like the business that it is in order to efficiently serve its congregation and community. Bills have got to be paid. There is a great chance that everyone who has contributed to the upkeep of doing ministry, will not always be financially compensated for their work. How ministries decide that varies, but that's none of your business. Everything that I am trying to impart in you is that when you're serving, God must be the number one priority. Your motives can never be about financial gain or status. You should be serving because your goal is to embody the heart of Christ, even when others around you don't. So, when you're serving in church, year after year and you never get paid, don't take it personally. It's not personal, and rarely ever is. If more of servants in ministry focused on the collaborative effort, the bigger picture, then the church could be more effective. This includes both pastors and servants. We inject our personal agendas to the worship environment, it's easy for money to be a distraction.

When you're serving, sure you'll most likely be doing things that you would be compensated for outside of the church, but that's not the point. When you're working in ministry you'll also learn new skills and trades and it's easy to forget that you're not there for that. I've found that church is often a breeding ground for entrepreneurs. People learn skills and start businesses as a result of things they've learned while serving. It's a suitable place for networking and sharing, but that's not why you're there.

Its easy for people to become disgruntled in their positions and reluctant to serve when we feel mishandled, especially as it relates to time and money. When you find yourself serving in church, several days a week and all-day Sunday, it starts to mimic a job, especially when you're tired or frustrated or broke. It's hard to serve and not get paid when your money is funny. Consider this, if you were a millionaire, would the fact that you aren't getting paid deter you from serving in ministry, for free? Nope. In fact, you'll not only be giving your time and talents, but you'll probably be dumping loads of money in your ministry as well. When you allow money, in excess or deficiency, to have a weighted role in your decision to serve, then you'll never reap the benefits intended in the process. Be clear about why you're serving and don't let money distract you. It's hard to give God your best when you're not serving yourself. It's easy to become complacent and stagnant. In the last few years, I've learned how to balance working on me behind the scenes while serving. I think the church lacks balance in so many ways. I feel like the root of it is the fear and a lack of faith. If you're not consciously serving one thing, then you're consciously serving another. If you're not focused on where you are than your attention is diverted. It can stand in the way of progress and where you're supposed to be.

We're so good at infiltrating our desires with God's will. We must know His will and know that He will fulfil our heart's desires. His will opens the door for us to do what we want. We get distracted with money and material things, trying to keep up with the Joneses rather than focusing on the purpose of the work. It's natural to have dreams and desires. It's also great to have ambitions, but you've got to align them with what He wants for you. If not, you'll get remnants and sprinkles of blessings, or a check or two, but still won't benefit fully, until you're obedient. It's so much easier to just do things His way the first time. Even when you don't want to, or don't understand His plan, it's easier to listen. I learned this lesson the hard way. I was serving someone, and I was so impatient that I moved before God told me to move and I missed a major opportunity. Sure, because of grace, I'll still have what God wants for me, but I could have had it much sooner.

Sometimes we get so consumed with money, that we inject ourselves in God's business. When you know God, and trust Him, you've got to reach a point where you settle in to His will for you. You have to reach a point when you realize that as much as you love yourself, that He loves you much more. Because of His love, the best is already waiting for you. You've just got to get out of the way, focus on the purpose and not the work and serving will be much easier to navigate. It usually won't seem practical, but you should trust the process.

When I'm most exhausted and depleted, it's natural to feel weary. Sometimes I just don't feel like doing anything at all. Once I make a commitment and say, "I'm doing it", I do. I am constantly checking myself about this because I never want to come across ungrateful. It's a struggle a times. As a servant leader, I've had days when I'm not on my A game, but I wasn't always fair to other people when they needed space. There are times when I'm moody and don't want to be bothered, but I'm reminded that someone out there wants what I have. It immediately shifts my posture and helps me to get my mind right. That is work. It's normal to have that disposition with a job, to expect someone to perform at 100 percent, because after all, they're being paid. The challenge is in selflessness and when you're working on auto pilot but have committed to serve in ministry. It's ok to be frustrated. I usually fuss and vent, but only with people who can redirect me. I believe that in your weakness, God gives you what you need. Sometimes the church teaches us not to feel like that, but I'm telling you its normal.

It's important to have people in your corner who will tell you the truth. No one will ever understand serving in the way that I do, but if they know me, they will always hold me accountable for my commitment to serve, even when I don't feel like working. We all think our opinions make sense, we think that it's the most accurate. But my feelings are just that, feelings. There is safety in a multitude of counsel and having honest people around me to hold me accountable, has made the difference. Between keeping real people around me and keeping my heart right, working and serving find balance.

I worked for a church for years and I played a very instrumental role in their growth. I was underpaid, I gave more than I should have, and honestly, I felt underappreciated. I was mistreated and verbally abused publicly when I was only carrying out the leader's wishes. I had to learn to identify what it was. I couldn't get it. I couldn't let being disgruntled make me quit. When I stopped doing the work of the job, I still served the ministry for another 3 years, because my assignment had not ended. I knew that if I left because of my emotions, I would be out of the will of God. The work for me had ended long before serving had. You still have to serve, even after you've given all you have, if God hasn't told you to leave. He wants your service to be altruistic.

This is why it's important to spend time with God. If I didn't know God's voice and what he was saying specifically to me, I would be lost. He knows my heart and I respond to that. He knows what I need, and I know that He honors my obedience. I'm not going to forfeit my blessings because I'm responding negatively to what someone did. Sometimes you have to serve, even when it doesn't align completely with how you feel. If God says serve, you cannot let your emotions get in the way, especially your emotions about money. Sometimes you may not agree with your leader, but you still have to cover them. You still have to ride with them. You're not serving them at all, you're serving God. The bad decisions of your leaders don't give you a free pass to stop serving. You still should serve in public and in private, even when it's tough. If I'm undergirding you and serving you, then I have to cover the covenant.

When you're only focused on the work, it's easy to create an internal narrative of bitterness. It's only been a few times that I've really had to question the assignment. I had to look at the situation both naturally and spiritually and pray. I looked at the non-financial benefits of serving. I'd be a millionaire if I had everything that the leaders have who I've served with. What I've gained is more valuable than money, its information, relationships and knowledge. Go learn, come home and teach. That was my assignment with Diddy. I initially went into the situation for work, but it was work that prepared me to serve my community. Working and serving in my life goes hand and hand. I worked a Hip Hop Music tour that opened the door to do a Country Music Tour with two of the largest country acts in the country. It was all because I obeyed and served.

I met a young woman recently who was serving in ministry and she shared with me her frustration about her ministry. Like most people serving in church, she was excited about the opportunity to serve her pastor and for years, she served with love and genuine compassion. She watched her pastor pay for work to be done in so many other areas in ministry but not hers. I've seen this happen far too often. She was watching other people get paid to do things she wasn't. Comparing her efforts to someone else's was the first mistake. Our pastors have a daunting task to not only feed the spirit man, but sometimes feed the bodies of the less fortunate in their church. Somewhere along the way, she had lost her focus. When I'm serving, I've learned not to look around into other people's stuff. The truth is that the pastor is the shepherd of the flock. The pastor is responsible. I don't know what God may be trying to work out in the life of another servant. I don't know what they may have gone through or what God has planned for them. It is never my job to try to stack my bricks up against someone else's rocks. I am not the authority on who deserves money now or who should get it later. That is God's decision.

I'll share with you the same thing I shared with her. Your faith should not be centered around your desire for the pastor to make the decision to pay you, your faith should be in God's ability to create increase. You should be so laser focused on your assignment that you don't have time to worry about what someone else is doing. The truth is that we're all God's children and we're all deserving of His love and favor. We can't let money make us envious or jealous. We can't be bitter about what God has done for someone else, instead we should rejoice and celebrate with them. When we go to school, our goal is to get a good grade so we can move on to the next level.

ISAAC CARREE

We should never be worried about what someone else's grade is. That's the teachers job. All we've got to be focused on is getting everything we came there for. You can't decide that it's time for you to get an A just because you feel like it. You certainly can't decide that you're ready to be rewarded just because someone else was. That's not your job and again it's not your business. When we serve, it's the same thing. We can't just decide that its time that we start getting paid because someone else is. You can't decide because your job is crazy, and your money is funny, that you should be paid to do what you committed to do on a voluntary basis.

The young woman learned a skill while serving in that ministry. She learned a skill that could help her to launch a business, but she didn't see that, she was looking at it the wrong way. A pastor from another state, was willing to pay her to do the same thing that she was doing at her home church. She looked at it and was insulted and frustrated. She looked at it and got angry. She felt like she shouldn't have to go to another church for them to value what she was doing for free at her church. She was missing her miracle. She couldn't see it. She couldn't see that God was doing more for her than giving her a pay check to run her ministry on Sundays, He was giving her a million-dollar business. Through serving, for free, she learned skills, strengthened weak places and was transforming from volunteer into a CEO.

How many of us have found ourselves in that same situation? I know I have. How many of us have overlooked the bigger picture and only focused on what we could see? I have. God was looking out for her in a way that was beyond her imagination. He didn't orchestrate heaven and earth so she could get a pay check at her church. He put her in that position to serve because He wanted to give her tools to build generational wealth. She should rejoice about not getting that pay check. Today, she serves ministries around the country, getting paid much more than a Sunday pay check, she'll make millions. She was a servant. She was rewarded as a servant. If she was a worker, her reward would have been a pay check. When God calls us to serve, He is not calling us to abuse us or to abandon our gifts.

When we say yes to serve, it is much different than responding to a classified or help wanted ad in the newspaper. When we say yes to serve, we're saying yes to purpose. So many of us get that wrong. Serving is not designed to be a lifetime sentence. It's the launching pad for your next. Whether that be your next assignment, or in the young woman's case, your next million-dollar business.

God gets more glory by having His servant as a millionaire, because we'll know what to do with it. We'll use it to build the body of Christ. We'll use it to glorify him. We will use it to serve, just in a bigger way. Do you think that God intends for only selfish and ungodly people to benefit from wealth? Absolutely not! He wants you to have it. He wants you to cash the check and deposit the savings bond. He just wants you to stand in the line, and wait. I'd hate to get up to the teller's window with someone else's check to cash. They may be ahead of me in the line, but I know what God promised me, and I can't take a chance and skip the line. I'll wait. I'll wait for what He has, just for me. I don't want a pay check from my church. I want several pay checks, from all around the world, so I can bring it back to my family, my community and yep, my church.

IT TAKES A VILLAGE

THE SERVANT LEADER

ISAAC CARREE

IT TAKES A VILLAGE
THE SERVANT LEADER

No one really knows the original author of the adage 'it takes a village to raise a child'. Some say it is an African proverb while others maintain the author to be from a Native American Tribe. Regardless of the origin, the adage has been used, modified, translated, and quoted in various languages, but the gist is the same. The original translation meant children, cannot be raised by parents alone. In its original format, it simply means that children are reared not only by their parents, but by every adult touching their lives. For example, bus drivers, teachers, doctors, and extended family members. As a child, I was raised to respect not only my parents but all adults, especially aunts, uncles and elders in the church. This level of respect was parallel to the expectation that those same adults would care for me whenever I was in their presence.

This principle of training and care has followed me throughout my life as a servant. If everyone we served with, shared the same values in team and village environments, we could all work together better. We would see the benefits of being accountable to one another. Those with more experience, are usually called to lead. This is where it gets difficult for the servant leader. Somewhere between adolescence and adulthood, we build a resistance to any form of authority. It's not that we don't value direction or mentorship, it's just that as the village concept left our families and communities, it also affected the way we handle authority. We want to do a great job when serving and we possess the ability to do a great job when we are serving, but when nurturing comes in the form of discipline or as a directive, we tend to shut down.

As servant leaders, it is important that we lead with the same posture that we served in. I have a small but efficient village. While I may lead them based on my assignment, I still serve with them, because we are serving a unified purpose. It's so easy for me to go about my day, sending emails, text messages and bothering them to death, so I am intentional about saying thank you. I am intentional about communicating wins with the team. I understand that because I serve them, the way that I lead is detrimental to the experiences they need to get while serving. If I lead outside of the team or village environment, and try to do things myself, then I not only affect my assignment, but theirs as well.

Leaders don't always adopt abusive leadership traits from ego or arrogance. Most of that behavior is learned and reciprocated, sometimes over generations. We learn as children to obey our elders. For the most part, they command and we react, either in submission or disobedience. As we mature some of our old habits remain. When a boss on a job or the leader of a ministry barks out a command, our initial reaction is to pump our brakes. So many of us operate from such dysfunctional levels of disobedience that we don't realize how ready we are to rebel. It's as if we travel back in time and become elder and child again? It is not unusual for us to complain, pout or act out, I know I'm guilty of it. Some of us act out by showing up late for appointments and practices, others by being sarcastic in meetings or condescending in tone. The bottom line here is that many of our actions toward each other, especially those who have been placed on our journey to challenge our growth, are simply reactions based on our relationship to team dynamics and authority figures.

The role of the servant leader is to be an authority. As an authority, the servant leader is expected to groom, train, love and correct those in the role of serving. The role of the person serving is simply to operate in the capacity of their gifts for the edification, or good, of the people and the overall purpose. We talked about understanding and knowing your purpose in an earlier chapter. When you aren't clear about your purpose, it is easy to be out of order and misunderstand our responsibilities inside the villages. Each person in the village has a specific role to play. In ministry, we understand that from the parking lot attendant to the choir member, each person's talent, skill and anointing, is needed to create the best experience in worship. It's the same thing on our jobs. The receptionist is just as important as the person on the production line. Every part of the village relies on another part to complete the task.

SERVICE MY WORDS. MY LIFE. MY TRUTH.

One aspect of village work, is building the team and learning when to lead and when to serve. Even good leaders have a problem delegating and accepting help. Building a village means trust and accountability. It's not a fan club or a fraternity. It is almost contradictory when those serving give so much push back when help is offered. I know, you're thinking that it depends on who's offering and what exactly could their intentions be. Honestly, we all have to be a little guarded about who we let attach to our purpose. However, if you're a servant leader, and your purpose involves serving, the type of people who will want to help, will only be servants, because that's what they've seen you do. A village represents strength.

Humility plays a critical part in the life of the servant leader. Being humble sometimes means placing yourself in the learner lane rather than the leader lane. It means being vulnerable. This is certainly easier said than done. Accepting help in some instances could very well mean that there may be some things that you might not know. There is no shame in leaning on your village. You are not the only one. I would like to share a paraphrased excerpt of an article found in the 2014 issue of the entrepreneurial magazine INC.com:

Consider some of the greatest leaders of our time, Abraham Lincoln, Theodore Roosevelt, Martin Luther King, Nelson Mandela, Oprah and the Dalai Lama, to name a few, all have something in common. They inspired people through sharing their failures and admitting they didn't have all the answers. These leaders were also openly grateful for the love and support of their circle and thus, attracted more of the same. They knew and understood they had a village supporting them on their journey. Leaders and servants who are aware, conscious, continuously growing personally, professionally, and who courageously ask for and openly receive support are stronger. What I like about the above excerpt more than anything else is the village reference. No one, regardless of who you are can do any work alone. We were created to interact. When we are vulnerable and ask for or accept help, a fundamental need is met. I believe that need in one, feeds the needs of the other.

Most challenges in serving can be attributed to misunderstandings that could have easily been avoided if purpose had been known.

Another aspect of village work is who makes up your village? When you do agree to give of yourself, recognize that a portion of your village will move into place immediately. Every person serving with you should be ready and available to do whatever it takes to get the job done. Each team player is valuable and should be operating at their best for the success of the entire team. While people have an innate drawing to power, its less important to identify a title, but what role each person will paly in the village. It would do you well to remember that just as you have a desire to serve, the people in your village have a similar desire to assist. As servants we should be flexible and as leaders we should accommodate new talent and mentor new servants. Refusing to expand your territory and reciprocate service, could prevent someone else from realizing their own purpose.

Let's talk about expanding your territory a bit. One of the things we are guilty of is non-selection by selection. What this means is when we are looking for team members and helpers, we look for the strongest, prettiest, most put together candidate. Sometimes its not even about their physical attributes but sometimes we choose the wrong people to serve with us because we pick based on personality and not purpose. If you open a restaurant you can hire a manager who can run the kitchen, handle orders and manage inventory well. They could even come to you with loads of experience but lack customer service and people skills. In the restaurant business, customer service is the bloodline of the business. I couldn't hire a manager who was great at everything but bad at handling customers. When serving, sometimes it is necessary to look for natural qualities that will help propel the purpose of the ministry or project.

As servant leaders, we have to express gratitude for your village. Being and showing thankfulness and affirming your village is important, especially when serving in ministry. Seek ways to show your village that they are not just needed but appreciated. It is expected that leaders extend gratitude. However, as mentioned earlier in this text, there are times when the servant becomes the leader when others are watching and growing. In these cases, it is not only necessary to be a great model but also to extend the example of graciousness. Let us be honest. Sometimes gratitude is difficult. We tend to want to extend gratitude when we classify the work as deserving. Help is help, solicited or otherwise and help is deserving of gratitude. Get this, gratitude begets grace. Actor Matthew McConaughey says of gratitude as he accepted the Oscar in 2014 "Gratitude is reciprocal". What he meant was you get what you give. Thankfulness is more than a feeling or state of mind, it is grace-invoking worship.

This village principle sounds good and does indeed work, when we allow it to. When we accept that our village is not a haphazard group of people but rather a design for our development and assistance, we move into a space that that helps us to grow. . We will find ourselves accepting constructive criticism and direction in addition to building life-long mentors and friends.

On the flip side when we do not allow the village principal to work in our lives the evidence shows up blaringly. We find ourselves in a perpetual stage of movement. No place seems worthy of our gifts. No one seems to understand the struggle we go through to serve. In the beginning, we might find solace in moving from place to place to serve, but at some point, even the movement becomes uncomfortable. I cannot say it enough. Being clear of ones' purpose provides the peace of being in the right place at the right time.

As we come to the end of this chapter let us review the components of our current village. Typically, personal villages include those we our friends, family and of course those who work along-side us in service. When evaluating our village, we should ask questions like, "am I challenged by my village? Is there a good mix of family, friends and co-laborers? What about the level of respect for each group's capacity to advise, share, help and learn"? Understanding the importance of villages makes it necessary to formulate a healthy one. Sometimes you may find that you will have to do a little pruning. If your village is stagnant, it is time to prune. If your village bears too much fruit on the same few trees, it is time to prune. Yes! Even farmers prune and chop limbs off good trees. If the fruit are too heavy, they will kill the tree. Such is your own village. Pruning can be painful, but it is always necessary at some point of growth.

I've listed a few key points around having a strong viable and needful village.

1. Never forget that your reactions in part come from your past. Be aware that the person on the other end has stuff too and neither of you know the others' story. Be kind as you go through the process of give and take with those within your village.

2. There is purpose in and for your life. Some of the most difficult people you will encounter are in place for your growth.

3. Be clear concerning your purpose. It is not for the master to dictate the journey but rather for the servant to proclaim.

4. Know your position. The catcher does not play the field.

5. Ask for what you need. Be bold. You are made that way!

6. Some of your village is given to you just because you committed to serve. Some of your village is chosen. Choose wisely.

7. Gratitude is critical and reciprocal. The more you give...the more you will get! Say thank you.

OUTSIDE
NOISE
UNECESSARY CHATTER

OUTSIDE NOISE
UNECESSARY CHATTER

I want to leave you with the lessons that I've learned about outside noise or what I fondly refer to as head trash. Head trash is the external noise that prohibits or impedes the mindset of serving. It is the stuff you think about or hear about that muddles the path of your journey. You know what I mean. The people around you who riddle you with their own ideas of how you should be giving your time, talents and money for the sake of ministry. I have heard it all. It seems when you are struggling yourself to understand the limits and boundaries of your servitude, it is at the precise moment that well-meaning family members will share their concern and worry that you are working too hard or too much. It is also during this time that those closest to you will begin to set forth questions and doubt that will have you asking yourself questions about your own reason for doing whatever it is that you committed to.

Questions such as are you being paid enough or should you be getting paid, especially if you are gifting your services as many of us do in ministry. What about your self-inflicted head trash? You have experienced it. We all have. This is where you have allowed yourself to work beyond what is healthy. You have failed to indulge in self-care which you know full well is necessary for anyone working in ministry and now you are tired. Fatigue becomes your new enemy. Being tired and allowing yourself to become run down opens the door to unclear thinking and confusion. This is the door that leads to your questioning your call to serve.

There are many times where the questioning is not the worst thing that could happen. The worst thing that could happen is staying in place while feeling neglected, used, or unappreciated. Leaders and servants who find themselves in this space are susceptible to feelings of inadequacy and self-loathing. Often it is in this space that life changing decisions are made; to either stay in place, complaining about being dissatisfied, or worse, to simply leave out of frustration.

As you can imagine, this space is debilitating to the servant leader. So, what do you do? How do you pull yourself up by the proverbial bootstraps and get back on track? Is it appropriate to give an answer to the naysayers? I think not!

Although the result of serving is a public manifestation, the purpose of serving is very private. It is necessary in these times to not only remember the why but also to seek the source. Most of us have heard the adage, 'from the horses' mouth'. Well, it is here that I suggest you go for answers. Just because God sends you, does not mean it will be easy. Just because your service is ordained, does not mean it will not be difficult. Just because you believe you are operating in your prophetic gift, does not mean that the heart of the people will be accepting. Thus, it is critical for the success of your commitment to remember the Who and Why of your service.

I learned two immutable precepts about managing the outside noise. The first was that sometimes you just got to be still and slow to vent to just anyone. Also, as difficult as it may be, make every attempt to maintain your integrity during your serving struggles. Refrain from sharing your negative experiences with naysayers is imperative. Let your conversations be respectful, honest and uplifting. Some of the same people I might have misjudged turned out to be the most instrumental on my journey. They now hold the elite position of friend in my life.

The second thing I learned during this journey is that every single person who touched my life in any way during every difficult time in my servant life left valuable impressions and lessons with me. They were each teaching tidbits that I needed along the way. Each lesson learned was needful for my tomorrow though I did not realize it at the time. Also, I might not have learned those invaluable lessons had I not had those experiences. It is much more difficult to eradicate the voices of loved ones because we trust them so. Sometimes even they will have a hard time understanding your calling and it is their intent to protect you even if it stifles you. It is these times that your resolve can only be maintained with clear purpose and vision.

While you may never completely drown out all of the outside noise in your servant life, you can certainly take comfort in knowing that regardless of doubt, insecurity and emotional hiccups, when your purpose is clear, it is easier to sit still. When your purpose is clear, it is a whole lot less stressful because you have the confidence that you are in the right place at the right time. When your purpose is clear, you are still moving forward.

My final thoughts as they relate to outside noise, is that things people say are not nearly as discouraging as what you say to yourself. Self-doubt and sabotage are far too common. Outside noise would be irrelevant if we had learned to trust our own instincts rather than internalizing and believing what we hear. We have all heard and read that there is power in our words. I would add that there is power in our thoughts. Believers understand this concept from the scriptures. It is possible for you to shush the naysayers and your own negative voice while maintaining your composure. The sure-win formula for quieting the outside noise is to push forward. Succeed. You can! The way to start is to first remember you have purpose. You are not operating for yourself. This is not your journey. It is the path toward your yes. Next, pray for continued guidance. It is okay to be frank with God. When you are unsure, ask. When you do not know, ask. Praying is your opportunity to not only commune with God but to also learn how to hear responses. Finally, understand that everything and everyone has been placed in and on your path for your good; even when you are unable to see it. I for one, love knowing that God knew the result of my journey through servanthood, at the beginning.

Let's talk about the unnecessary chatter of self-sabotage. Self-sabotage is simply embracing as truth anything that is detrimental to one's self. From something someone tells us about ourselves, to prior failures, and even how we look, if it does not align with our purpose we must consider it trash. It takes practice to move through self-sabotage to get to a place where we recognize our true selves. The first step is to evaluate the sabotaging thoughts for exactly what they are. Instead of searching for the truth in them, first seek to dispel them. If you cannot, then trust it as truth. If you can honestly discard the trash, then it is not factual, and you must separate yourself from it. Here is an example; someone says you never finish anything and that you are a quitter. The solution, instead of owning this statement simply because someone knows of a few times you have stopped and not finished, look at the situation and determine the real reason you started and the real reason you stopped. That will be your truth. That is what you will accept. Nothing more and nothing less. Once you know your truth, it is not necessary to prove anything to anyone. It is not necessary to challenge your adversary. It is only necessary that you know and own your own truth. This will minimize the head trash. No, it will not take it away, but it will make it inconsequential. Repeat this process every time you find yourself saying no to yourself. Every time you hear that little nagging voice that insists you can't do it, or it's not for you. Process the why and only own what remains as truth. Self-sabotage will stop.

The other annoying outside noise can come from your own desires. Looking at others and comparing yourself can leave you feeling like you do not measure up. The truth is you are exactly where you are supposed to be. You have exactly what you are supposed to have. Each person has a definitive path and what and how they acquire the stuff as they go along is up to God. It is a myth to believe that the speed of your success is contingent on how good you are. Blessings are from God. This explains why the Joneses look so successful. Here's a tidbit for you, you look super successful to the Joneses too. It turns out that all grass looks greener from a distance!

Remember that hurts, naysayers, self- doubt, past failures, the failures of others, and the criticism of others breed exhaustion, poor health, empty busyness and feelings of despondency. Understand how to identify the difference between noise and sound. Noise is trash, sound is music. Living and dealing in the present moment helps us to avoid imaginary obstacles. Move through the fear of making the same mistakes others have made. Know that something will always be different for you. Steal time for self-healing and recuperating. Never forget that the frequency you tune in to determines whether you will hear noise or sound. It is always your choice.

FROM MY HEART
A SERVANT'S HEART

There is not a day that I haven't received positive messages about my work. I hear your stories, and they push me to serve more. I want to reach everyone. It's natural to want to quit and to try to do it all your way by yourself. What makes you do it one more day, one more assignment. Prioritizing is the best way to keep those feeling from slipping in, but if they do, I think about my assignment to you. To my public, to bring you my best. When you remember you, while you serve others, the balance will give you peace. I've had to learn this because it's essential in staying on point. You'll always have to work you. Because I serve, work is always available. There are people who work on their jobs for 30 and 40 years. I think it's because they found balance. Somewhere, somehow found a rhythm. They found a happy place to keep going day after day. I am searching for that balance. In finding what works for me, I prioritize, create balance, make time for me.

As a servant, there will be so many things that you'll have to step away from and come back to. My mind is always thinking about what next. We start and stop projects and its ok. It's about God's timing. Sometimes we're afraid to pull the trigger and stay the course of the assignment, it's easier said than done. Most people procrastinate because of fear. Whether it's money to fulfill the business, failure, and the feeling of being overwhelmed. Serving has expanded my knowledge of who God is.

What I've learned most is just how faithful God is. When you're serving and the position you're in is a supplemental role, it can look like backward steps. For me, every door that I've ever gone through and every check that I've ever made has been through serving. It's never been because my voice is so good, it's because I've been faithful. People call me because they've witnessed my posture, it hasn't at all been because I've asked for the opportunity. I don't serve for reciprocation. I am serving to give to someone else.

I recognized that God opens the door. People may be the vehicle, but soon they'll forgot about how good you are, but God won't. Here are a few things I want you to take away from this book:

Serving is not a job, it's a privilege! When you serve with the right spirit and a pure heart God will exalt you. Don't allow pride to stand in the way of someone helping you reach your destiny. The quickest route to God's best for your life is through obedience. Don't allow anyone to control you or abuse you, know how to identify that controlling abusive leader and RUN! It's toxic and that's not what serving is about. Never lose who you are while serving someone else, but at the same time don't expect the one you're serving to put you on, that's God's job!

Make sure the people you serve can trust you. Remember, you hear a lot, see a lot and experience a lot so don't forfeit your opportunity by judging them or running your mouth. Make sure at all times, you cover them, God will honor that! God has blessed me in these 28 years, not because I'm so good nor because of my ability, I've been blessed because I've been found faithful serving! Don't serve for opportunity, status, money, or for someone to give you a platform. Serve because you've been called to sow into someone else's life! Serve unto God, I promise you and I'm a living witness all those things will come.

This journey was not easy nor was it always fun, but it was necessary! I'm a better man because of my service unto the Lord! So I pray this book has given you some insight on the importance of serving. I pray this book can help navigate you through some rough seasons of your life. And I pray that this book will unlock your destiny and set you up for what God has already prepared for you! You've been served! My Words. My Life. My Truth.

Isaac Carree

ISAAC
CARREE
THE SERVANT

ISAAC, CARREE
THE SERVANT

With over 28 years in the music industry, Isaac Carree got his start as a celebrated soloist for some of gospel music's greats. Sharing the stage with John P. Kee and the New Life Community Choir, Isaac co-founded the award winning contemporary gospel group, Men of Standard. For over 10 years, they toured, recorded five albums and released several numbers hits. In 2011 Isaac released his first solo album entitled, Uncommon Me. Reset, his sophomore project was released under his independent label, Door 6 Entertainment. Both solo albums debuted at number one Billboard's gospel music charts.

In addition to achieving success as a solo artist, Isaac has toured with Steve Harvey, Kirk Franklin, Mary Mary, The Kingsmen Tour, The Festival of Praise Tour, the Bad Boy Reunion Tour and The Soul 2 Soul Tour with Faith Hill and Tim McGraw. Throughout his career Isaac has performed on television and on stages around the world. He is the recipient of a myriad of awards including, BMI, ASCAP and the prestigious Stella Awards. Isaac's gifts on stage transparently demonstrates the power of God's restoration. He wants listeners and readers to relate and be inspired by his songs and words of the redemptive power of God's love.

In addition to the release of his debut book, **Service: My Words. My Life. My Truth.**, Isaac is hosting a conference, The Plug to share with young and aspiring artists, keys on how to navigate and build a career of longevity and of purpose. With more music and projects on the way, Isaac Carree is a beacon of light and hope. He wants to share with the world the message, that it's never too late to start again.

Made in the USA
Middletown, DE
21 November 2017